COPENHAGEN '92-'93 ON $50 A DAY

by Alice Garrard

PRENTICE HALL TRAVEL

NEW YORK • LONDON • TORONTO • SYDNEY • TOKYO • SINGAPORE

FROMMER BOOKS

Published by Prentice Hall General Reference
A division of Simon & Schuster Inc.
15 Columbus Circle
New York, NY 10023

ISBN 0-13-334707-9
ISSN 1055-5358

Design by Robert Bull Design
Maps by Geografix Inc.

Manufactured in the United States of America

FROMMER'S COPENHAGEN ON $50 A DAY '92–'93

Editor-in-Chief: Marilyn Wood
Senior Editors: Judith de Rubini, Pamela Marshall, Amit Shah
Editors: Alice Fellows, Paige Hughes, Theodore Stavrou
Assistant Editors: Suzanne Arkin, Peter Katucki, Lisa Renaud, Ellen Zucker
Managing Editor: Leanne Coupe

CONTENTS

LIST OF MAPS

COPENHAGEN

COPENHAGEN WALKING TOURS

OUTSIDE COPENHAGEN

INVITATION TO THE READERS

In researching this book, I have come across many wonderful establishments, the best of which I have included here. I am sure that many of you will also come across wonderful hotels, inns, restaurants, guest houses, shops, and attractions. Please don't keep them to yourself. Share your experiences, especially if you want to comment on places that have been included in this edition that have changed for the worse. You can address your letters to:

Alice Garrard
Frommer's Copenhagen on $50 A Day '92–'93
c/o Prentice Hall Travel
15 Columbus Circle
New York, NY 10023

A DISCLAIMER

Readers are advised that prices fluctuate in the course of time and travel information changes under the impact of the varied and volatile factors that affect the travel industry. Neither the author nor the publisher can be held responsible for the experiences of readers while traveling. Readers are invited to write to the publisher with ideas, comments, and suggestions for future editions.

SAFETY ADVISORY

Whenever you're traveling in an unfamiliar city or country, stay alert. Be aware of your immediate surroundings. Wear a moneybelt and keep a close eye on your possessions. Be particularly careful with cameras, purses, and wallets, all favorite targets of thieves and pickpockets.

CHAPTER 1

INTRODUCING COPENHAGEN

Upbeat, arty, and perenially popular with the young, that's Copenhagen. Visitors to the city particularly love Tivoli and the statue of the Little Mermaid, the symbol of Copenhagen, and to join the crowds milling along Strøget, the city's great pedestrian street. The jazz capital of Europe, Copenhagen pulses with music. Its Royal Theater is a showcase for dance, theater, and opera; its streets, living museums of architecture and history. This is a university city and has been since 1479. Today Copenhagen's Huset (meaning "house") still welcomes young residents and visitors, catering to their needs and providing space for music, art, and socializing. A happy-go-lucky place, Copenhagen will welcome you warmly and its charms will linger in your memory long after you leave.

1. GEOGRAPHY, HISTORY & BACKGROUND

GEOGRAPHY

Lively Copenhagen spreads out over two flat islands—Zealand and Amager—in the 13-mile wide Øresund (the Sound), at the entrance to the Baltic Sea. The main part of the city lies on the larger island Zealand (spelled *Sjaelland* in Danish); and the rest of the city, including Copenhagen Airport, lies on the smaller island of Amager. Several bridges connect these two islands.

Modern Copenhagen, which is home to a third of Denmark's population, resembles an outstretched left hand, palm up; the old part of the city is the palm, with fingers of development reaching south and west. The city has grown so much in recent years, however, that the fingers have taken on a webbed look. Strøget (it means "the

WHAT'S SPECIAL ABOUT COPENHAGEN

Strøget

- ☐ World-class shopping and great street performers.

Tivoli

- ☐ Aglow with 100,000 light bulbs, fireworks, and merriment.

Sculpture

- ☐ The Little Mermaid, at the water's edge on Langelinie.
- ☐ Hans Christian Andersen, with top hat and cane, in the west corner of Town Hall Square.
- ☐ Lur Blowers, playing ancient Scandinavian instruments.

Fountains

- ☐ Gefion Fountain, depicting a goddess plowing the island of Zealand from Sweden.
- ☐ The Dragon Fountain, which dominates Town Hall Square.
- ☐ Caritas Fountain, on Gammel Torv, Denmark's only remaining Renaissance well.
- ☐ Stork Fountain, on Strøget at Amagertorv.

Steeples

- ☐ The Bourse, with its dragon-tail steeple.
- ☐ Church of Our Savior, with its outside staircase.

Museums

- ☐ National Museum, with gold amulets from the Viking period and lurs, 3,000-year-old Scandinavian instruments.
- ☐ Ny Carlsberg Glyptotek, for its collection of ancient sculptures and engaging modernists.
- ☐ State Museum for Fine Art, Denmark's largest art museum.
- ☐ Louisiana Museum of Modern Art, Denmark's world-class and most visited museum.

Palaces-Castles

- ☐ Rosenborg—home of the crown jewels, and a jewel itself, set in a beautiful park.
- ☐ Christiansborg—with 800 years of history and impressive state rooms.
- ☐ Frederiksborg, in Hillerød, the "Versailles of Northern Europe."
- ☐ Kronborg, in Helsingør, Hamlet's castle in Shakespearean lore.

Events/Festivals

- ☐ Copenhagen Jazz Festival, beginning of July.
- ☐ Copenhagen Summer (classical music) Festival, three weeks in July.

For the Kids

- ☐ Tivoli.
- ☐ Legoland, a playful pilgrimage for small fry.

After Dark

- ☐ Jazz clubs downtown and in Nørrebro.
- ☐ The Royal Theater, with ballet, opera, and theater under one roof.

Street"), a mile-long pedestrian thoroughfare since 1962, cuts through the heart of the old part of town.

A cosmopolitan city in a largely argricultural country, Copenhagen is the second-largest Scandinavian city and the capital of the smallest of the three Scandinavian countries. Denmark is comparable in size to Connecticut and Massachusetts combined, but more like Maine in climate. On the same latitude as Moscow and Ketchikan, Alaska, Copenhagen is blessed with a milder climate thanks to the Gulf Stream. Temperatures average 32 degrees F in January, and 64 degrees F in July. It is a land totally surrounded by and at peace with the water, and though there are no mountains or rivers, the sea is never more than 30 miles away.

The ferry link between Denmark and what is now Sweden at Helsingør, 30 miles north of Copenhagen, has existed since the 1400s. There is another ferry link with Malmö, Sweden.

PEOPLE

In Copenhagen, many people speak English like natives. Older Danes may not be as conversant as their children, nor have they seen as many American movies, which proliferate in Copenhagen. Danish schoolchildren study English for four years, starting in elementary school. (I visited a fifth-grade English class, and the kids' favorite topic of conversation was Disneyland.) School is compulsory for 7 years, but most children go for 12. Students get a free physical and dental exam every year. If they continue to study at the university level, although they do not pay tuition, they are responsible for room and board, which mounts up quickly—as you'll see. At age 18, a Dane can vote and drink. *Registering* for military service is compulsory for men, though they may never actually be required to serve.

Danes work a 37-hour week and receive five weeks' paid vacation a year. Skilled workers earn $47,000 a year; unskilled workers, $35,000; the minimum wage is $12 an hour, and those who are laid off get one year's unemployment. Don't expect to find Danish workers sitting behind a desk after 5pm. They're off enjoying nature, often sailing since they have a special bond with the water. And it's been said that Danes are born on bikes.

They are a cordial people, generous with their time and quick to offer guests congenial conversation and a cup of coffee. I expected to find a race of tall men and women, but encountered many people, women especially, at or near my eye level, just over five feet.

More than half the Danes own their own homes. Their life-style depends on two incomes, and 40% of the work force is made up of women; 70% of Danish children ages 3 to 5 go to day-care programs during the day. The divorce rate unfortunately mirrors that of the United States: Two out of every three marriages fail.

Growing old is not so bad in Denmark; the elderly are respected and treated with dignity. At age 67, every citizen receives a national pension, and senior citizens are encouraged and aided with social programs to spend the last years of their lives at home rather than in a nursing home or hospital.

Devoted to peace, the Danish people remained neutral during World War I. They endured Nazi occupation during World War II. Most of the Danish Jews and refugees from other countries survived because of their country's strong Resistance movement.

The Danes hold liberal and compassionate views on many social issues including homosexuality. For example, both "common law" marriages and civil gay marriages called "registered partnerships" are recognized by the state, which grants the couples in such unions many of the same rights and benefits as other more traditional married couples.

As independent and free-spirited as the Danes are, it surprises me, a New Yorker, that they don't indulge in a little innocent jaywalking. But they are a law-abiding folk—and jaywalking *is* a finable offense—so I had to hold my natural impulses in check. When in Denmark . . .

The hefty taxes (40% to 60%) placed on Danish citizens entitle them to free medical, dental, and hospital care, university tuition, a pension at age 67, and a retirement home if they choose one. The ever-joking Danes claim that the four figures writhing in pain at the main entrance to the Parliament building represent the Danish taxpayers—actually they symbolize headache, earache, stomach-ache, and toothache, but I can't say why.

Christmas Eve is a time of great celebration for the Danes—the country's goose population drops dramatically. Candles glow on fresh evergreen trees, and there is dancing, singing, and gift giving. According to an old Danish song, "The Christmas season lasts until Easter." Christmas is celebrated at home, but New Year's Eve is rung in along Strøget and in the city's restaurants. Danes celebrate their queen's birthday on April 16, and school kids get the day off to wave flags in front of her palace. On June 23, Midsummer's Eve, Danes head for the nearest beach (in Copenhagen, that's Bellevue) and burn bonfires long into the night.

HISTORY

Denmark is the oldest existing monarchy in the world; its flag, the oldest existing flag. Human beings have occupied the site on which Copenhagen stands for the past 6,000 years, and the city itself has existed in one form or another since the year A.D. 1000, when it was a fishing village called Havn

DATELINE

- **1167** Bishop Absalon establishes a fort on the present site of Copenhagen to protect a ferry route across the Øresund.

(continues)

DATELINE

- **1254** Copenhagen receives a charter.
- **1443** Copenhagen becomes the capital of Denmark.
- **1479** The University of Copenhagen is established.
- **1536** Lutheranism becomes the official religion of Denmark.
- **1658–60** Wars with Sweden result in Denmark's losing one-third of its land holdings.
- **1670** Kongens Nytorv is constructed.
- **1711** Bubonic plague kills 20,000 people, one-third of the population.
- **1728** Fire destroys 40% of the houses in the city and several public buildings.
- **1748** The Royal Theater is established at Kongens Nytorv.
- **1775** The Royal Copenhagen Porcelain Factory is founded.
- **1794** The original Christiansborg Palace is almost totally destroyed by fire.
- **1795** Another fire

(continues)

(meaning "harbor"). The catch, then as now, was mainly herring.

Little is known about Denmark's history before the Viking period dating from A.D. 800 to 1050. Warring people (among themselves as well as with other nations), the Vikings raided and plundered far and wide, leaving their mark (and some descendants) in England, Germany, Sweden, Norway, Russia, Iceland, and Greenland. Canute the Great, who later converted to Christianity, reigned over Denmark and England simultaneously from 1017 to 1035.

The Vikings were, perhaps, the first world travelers, and the Danes have inherited their wanderlust. More Danes live in the United States now than in all of Denmark. Except for Canute the Great, the Vikings would probably be mortified to see what staunch humanitarians and peace lovers their descendants have become.

In 1167, Bishop Absalon, a charismatic leader who was both a man of the cloth and of the sword, established a castle here to protect the ferry route across the Øresund to the Skanör peninsula (now Sweden). During this time, the town was protected by moats and earthworks (some of them can still be seen around Christianshavn); high walls were added later. Thus fortified, the town held potential invaders—mainly the Swedes—at bay. The only way to enter the town was through one of four guarded gates, which were demolished, along with most of the ramparts, in the mid-18th century. The town was chartered in 1254.

As the community expanded into a trading center, so did its name, from Havn to København, or "Merchants' Harbor." From 1250 to 1820, fires, wars, and epidemics ravaged the town and its population, but in characteristic resiliency, Copenhagen survived each in turn to flourish again.

A TIME OF GROWTH

Copenhagen did not become the cultural center of Denmark until the 15th century; prior to that the seat of culture was in the older town of Roskilde, 20 miles to the west. But in 1440, the Danish king, Christoffer of Bavaria, moved the royal residence to Copenhagen, dramatically changing the city's history. Three years later, Copenhagen was officially named the capital of Denmark, and the University of Copenhagen—so much a part of city life today—was founded in 1479.

Copenhagen remained a walled city from the twelfth century until the mid-19th century, and the land lying outside the walls was used for pasture. When Tivoli opened in 1843, it was in the country, outside the walls. The present-day streets of Vestervoldgade, Nørre Voldgade, and Gothersgade mark where the moat-fronted ramparts once stood. The modern city is built on streets laid out in the late 14th century, which accounts for their unexpected twists and turns. Visit the City Museum on Vesterbrogade in summer to see the large outdoor model that shows what the city looked like in 1530.

Christian IV, one of the country's best known and revered kings, lived from 1588 to 1648. He succeeded his father at the young age of 11 but was not crowned until he was 19. His dream was to transform Copenhagen into Scandinavia's most beautiful city (and, indeed, he came close). Most of the city's striking buildings were erected during his reign: the Stock Exchange with its unique dragon-tail spire; the Round Tower, a combination of church tower and observatory; Christianshavn, an expansion of the city intended as a separate town for merchants and set up in Dutch fashion with canals; and the stunning Frederiksborg

DATELINE

destroys many buildings.

- **1801** Denmark and England fight a major naval battle outside Copenhagen during the Napoleonic Wars. Copenhagen's population is 100,000.
- **1807** England lays seige to Copenhagen and captures the Danish naval fleet, then the second largest in Europe.
- **1813** Søren Kierkegaard is born in Copenhagen.
- **1814** At the Vienna Congress, Norway—ruled by Denmark for more than four centuries—is united with Sweden.
- **1819** Hans Christian Andersen arrives in Copenhagen from Odense at age 14.
- **1843** Tivoli opens.
- **1844** The first folk high school opens.
- **1847** The first rail connection in Denmark is made between Copenhagen and Roskilde.
- **1849** The monarchy is changed from absolute to constitu-

(continues)

DATELINE

tional; the royal castles become state property.

- **1853** Cholera outbreak kills more than 5,000 people.
- **1856** The ramparts of the old city are removed.
- **1864** Denmark loses Schleswig and Holstein to Germany after a war.
- **1884** Rebuilt Christiansborg Palace burns again.
- **1892** Electricity is first used in Copenhagen.
- **1894** Copenhagen becomes a free port.
- **1900** The population numbers 400,000.
- **1905** A striking new town hall is built opposite Tivoli.
- **1911** The main railway station moves to its present site on Vesterbrogade.
- **1913** The Little Mermaid statue is installed at Langelinie.
- **1914–18** Denmark remains neutral during World War I.
- **1915** Danish women get the vote.

(continues)

Castle at Hillerød in North Zealand. Under King Christian IV's influence, the city almost doubled in size. For good reason, he is called the Builder King, although "not renowned for his parsimony," which created fiscal problems for his successor.

When the Round Tower was completed in 1642, the king could not resist riding on horseback up the spiral ramp to the top of it; legend has it that in 1721, Peter the Great of Russia, on a visit to Copenhagen, would do the same thing, followed by the Czarina in a carriage drawn by six horses.

The 17th and 18th centuries were particularly trying ones for Copenhagen. The Swedes attempted to invade twice, in 1658 and 1660. They took over Kronborg Castle in Helsingør, and by the time the warring ceased, one-third of Denmark had been ceded to Sweden. The bubonic plague struck in 1711, killing 20,000 people, a third of the city's population.

FIRES, PLAGUES & WARS

In 1728, a huge fire broke out and engulfed the narrow streets, destroying 40% of the houses and some public buildings as it spread. In 1794 fire struck again; this time, Christiansborg Palace went up in flames, leaving only the royal stables and the court theater standing. The next year, another fire destroyed more houses and churches; however, the plucky population rebuilt their city and grew in number.

A notorious incident in Danish royal history occurred during the reign of Christian VII. The king was insane, and from 1770 to 1772, the country was actually ruled by his German physician, Johann Freidrich Struensee, who enacted many reforms and didn't perform too badly, until he made the mistake of having an affair with the queen.

The poor man lost his head in more ways than one.

During the Napoleonic Wars, England attacked the neutral Denmark in the fierce Battle of Copenhagen Sound in 1801, in which Danish Crown Prince Frederik VI, acting in behalf of his father, the above-mentioned insane Christian VII, was forced to surrender. Six years later, the British forces returned, and under the command of Lord Nelson, bombarded civilian areas of Copenhagen for five days, destroying much of the city, including the cathedral and the area around the university. Again, Crown Prince Frederik VI surrendered, and this time the English sailed off with the prized Danish fleet, a fact that sets Danish teeth on edge to this day.

King Frederik VII, known as *foklekær* or "people-beloved," initiated the shift from absolute to constitutional monarchy in Denmark in 1849, after Denmark had been an absolute monarchy for more than 100 years. At this time, Copenhagen was the only big town in a country populated mainly with poor peasants in small villages. This would soon change.

In the middle of the 19th century the city was beginning to grow again, when a cholera epidemic claimed 5,000 lives. In 1884 Christiansborg Palace burned for the second time. (The third palace—the one you see today—was built around 1900.) One bright spot during this period was the opening in 1843 of an entertainment park called Tivoli outside the city walls.

MODERN DENMARK

Moving into the 20th century, Denmark was not involved in World War I but was greatly affected by World War II, when the Nazis occupied Copenhagen from 1940 to 1945. The plucky, outraged country

DATELINE

- **1920** Influenza outbreak kills more than 3,000.
- **1925** Copenhagen Airport, originally called Kastrup, opens on Amager island (it is expanded in 1937).
- **1934** The S-tog railway begins service.
- **1940–45** Germany occupies Copenhagen; Resistance movement created.
- **1943** Seven thousand Danish Jews are smuggled into Sweden.
- **1944** The Nazis blow up part of Tivoli.
- **1962** Strøget becomes a pedestrian thoroughfare.
- **1964** The Little Mermaid is decapitated at Langelinie; a replacement head is quickly made.
- **1971** The counterculture community of Christiania takes root in Christianshavn.
- **1972** Margrethe II is crowned queen of Denmark, the country's first female monarch, and at 32, the world's youngest.

(continues)

DATELINE

- **1973** Denmark joins the Common Market, the only Scandinavian country to do so.
- **1990** Tycho Brahe planetarium, the largest in Western Europe, opens.
- **1991** Rungstedlund, home of author Karen Blixen, opens to the public.

proved an inhospitable place. The Danish king, Christian X, was arrested in 1943 and martial law was declared in the small country.

The Resistance movement saved the lives of most of the Danish Jews, some 7,000 of whom were smuggled into neutral Sweden in October 1943. Instrumental in this effort was Niels Bohr, physicist, Nobel Prize–winner, and part of a resistant group called the Sewing Circle. Bohr himself barely escaped to Sweden and relocated to Great Britain and the United States for the duration of the war, during which time he met with both Churchill and Roosevelt in his own unflagging peace efforts.

Only 53 Danish Jews died at the hands of the Nazis, and those who returned to Denmark after the war received all their homes and possessions back (this was not the case in every European country). At the end of the occupation, on a May evening, the citizens of the city stripped their windows of black curtains, replacing them with lighted candles, and decorated their bicycles with flowers. Mindelunden, a memorial park to honor Danish civilians who lost their lives during the occupation, was established north of the central city.

In 1949 a small, international group met in Askov, Denmark, and founded an organization called Servas that echoes the words of the refrain, "Let there be peace on earth, and let it begin with me." *Servas* is an Esperanto word meaning "to serve," and the premise of the organization is that if individuals from different cultures get to know each other, they will be less likely to bear arms against one another. By visiting in one another's homes, they can better understand one another—to acknowledge the similarities and respect the differences. Today Servas has 69 hosts in Copenhagen, 250 in Denmark, and 12,622 worldwide (see "Home Stays or Visits," Chapter 2).

The small but strong-willed country refuses to attack another country, but will defend its own, if need be. It rigidly adheres to a

IMPRESSIONS

There is nothing of Hamlet in their nature.
—R. H. BRUCE LOCKHART, *My Europe*, 1952

IMPRESSIONS

If I were a dictator, I would not occupy Denmark for fear of being laughed to death.

—JOHN STEINBECK

"no-nukes" policy. With the discovery of oil and gas in the North Sea, 90% of its oil, gas, and energy needs are met.

CHRISTIANIA — A SOCIOCULTURAL EXPERIMENT

In 1971, squatters took over empty army barracks on Christianshavn, and the countercultural community of Christiania was born. Many Copenhageners see it as a blight and a haven for drug addicts, ne'er-do-wells, and criminals. Most call it off-putting and steer visitors clear of it; some (particularly visitors) find it compelling, if only from a sociocultural perspective. The population of former hippies has aged; many are parents with ever-increasing responsibilities; a few are grandparents to the third generation of Christianians.

POLITICS

In 1849, a constitutional monarchy, Europe's oldest, was established in Denmark, and democracy took root. Legislative authority rests equally with the crown and parliament. Parliament, which sits in Copenhagen, has one chamber, called the *Folketing,* with 179 members, including two from the Faroe Islands and two from Greenland, both autonomous parts of the kingdom of Denmark. Members of parliament are elected for four-year terms by citizens 18 years and older.

Election time can be dicey, since the country now has a *multi*party system (it had four parties until 1973). With about a dozen parties, just imagine the quantity of election speeches. Over the years of political changes and skirmishes, the most powerful party has

---

IMPRESSIONS

. . . This long wonderful woman . . . just cannot contain herself and cannot remain quiet. . . . And under that maternal air, the stirring of a restlessness, a vehemence, an intellect, a searching for answers.

—DESCRIPTION OF QUEEN MARGRETHE II
BY DANISH AUTHOR THORKILD HANSEN

remained the Social Democrats, supported primarily by middle-class workers and farmers. It has 33% representation in parliament; parties with more than 10% representation include the Conservatives, Socialist People's Party, and Liberals; Center Democrats and Progressives have 8% to 9% representation. It makes for lively debate.

The monarch (Queen Margrethe II) presides over a 19-member State Council of ministers, headed by the Prime Minister, whom she appoints with the approval of parliament. She must sign all laws passed by the parliament. Parliament is in session from September to April, and the queen is usually in residence at Amalienborg Palace during that time. A flag flying outside the castle attests to her presence.

THE ARTIST QUEEN

Queen Margrethe II is the latest monarch in a unbroken succession that goes back to the first Danish kings in the 10th century. Born in 1940, she is also the world's youngest queen and a striking and accomplished one who has vehemently shunned being "a spectator to life."

Fluent in seven languages, she is a recognized artist who has designed everything from stamps, book covers, furniture, Christmas seals, chasubles (the outer garment worn by priests at mass), and the costumes for a television production of a Hans Christian Andersen story. She also illustrated an edition of J. J. R. Tolkien's *The Lord of the Rings*. Her lithographic prints are sold at the airport, among other places. She and her husband, Prince Henrik, translated Simone de Beauvoir's novel *All Men Are Mortal* into Danish; the queen also designed the book's cover.

Margrethe met Count Henrik, a dashing French diplomat, when she was studying abroad. They courted for a couple of years and married in a fairy-tale ceremony in 1967; she was 27 and he, 33. Within four years she had had two sons—Crown Prince Frederik in 1968 and Prince Joachim in 1969—and had become the queen of Denmark, the first official female monarch the country has ever known. She was able to accede to the throne because of a law approving female succession instituted by her father in 1953.

Any photographs of the tall, handsome couple reveal the obvious affection they have for one another. As real as they are regal, they, along with Juan Carlos and Sophia of Spain, are Europe's most striking royal couple.

Margrethe is, with King Hans, only the second Danish monarch not named Christian or Frederik since the 15th century. She places the II after her name out of deference to another Margrethe who ruled Denmark (a kingdom that would expand under her rule to include Norway and Sweden) as regent from 1375 until her death in

1412; her father, Valdemar IV, died leaving no direct heirs, only children who had to grow up before they could rule. Margrethe did the job—and quite capably, in spite of taunts like "King Pantless."

The present-day monarch's powers are limited primarily to signing all legislature into the law. For dispensing her royal duties, Margrethe II receives an annual salary of about $5,900,000, tax-free. Out of it, she pays a staff of 130 people, the pensions of former employees, her own travel expenses, and the cost of renovations to the interiors of Amalienborg and Fredenborg palaces, her two official residences.

Like Christian IV before her, this highly respected monarch could be called a builder, not of architectural monuments but of the trust and admiration of her people, who look to her not only as a leader but as a role model. If the monarchy were abolished tomorrow and Margrethe ran for president, she'd win.

SOME CULTURAL BACKGROUND

DESIGN Denmark is known for its design sense, particularly of furniture, china, crystal, and cutlery that is both functional and beautiful. Homes around the world have been enhanced by creations by Royal Copenhagen Porcelain, founded in 1775; Bing & Grondahl, founded in 1853; and Georg Jensen's Silversmithy, founded in 1904.

In the forefront of furniture design since the 1920s, Danish designers have often taken existing designs (a Windsor chair, say) and adapted them to a Danish esthetic, or they create something totally unique: "The Ant," a chair by architect/designer Arne Jacobsen, with a back and seat of molded wood on spindly steel legs, has been reproduced by the thousands. Jacobsen's chairs "The Swan" and "The Egg" also inspire instant recognition. Besides showing up in offices and homes around the world, his designs and those of other Danes have also become museum pieces.

Poul Henningsen's PH lamps are well known in Denmark. The "Artichoke" is aptly named, and other designs resemble spacecraft or exotic blossoms. The light bulb in Henningsen's lamps is fairly well hidden by the shade, but it manages to illumine just the same.

Georg Jensen, whose name is a household word because of his internationally recognized silversmithy, was a sculptor who rechanneled his talents to jewelry and cutlery design. When he died in 1935, the *New York Times* declared him the greatest silver artist in 300 years.

THE PERFORMING ARTS The Royal Theater was established at Kongens Nytorv in 1748. It remained under court patronage for 100 years, at which time the Ministry of Cultural Affairs took over. Unique in its staging of ballet, opera, and theater under one roof, it rarely has a night without a performance.

Films have been made in Denmark since the dawn of the genre, beginning with a couple of short documentaries made by the royal court photographer in 1897. From 1906 to 1910, 125 films poured forth each year, compared to 20 today. During the 1920s, the comedy team of Long and Short were Denmark's Laurel and Hardy. Modern Danish films, which can be quite moving, deal with life, often of the middle class, as it is lived outwardly and inwardly.

EDUCATION Denmark's first folk high school was founded in 1844 by theologian N. F. S. Grundtvig, who believed that curiosity and the desire to learn are the only real motivation in educating people. Unorthodox for the time, the schools, for people 18 and older, required no entrance exams or final exams, and the curriculum was large and varied. Today there are more than 90 folk high schools in Denmark, including one in English. Multitalented Grundtvig also wrote 35% of the Danish hymnal.

Danes devour the printed word, and their homes overflow with books. Sixty newspapers are published in this small country; among the most popular in Copenhagen are *Politiken* for news and *B.T.* and *Esktrabladet* for gossip and comics.

RELIGION Like its other Scandinavian brethren, Denmark is primarily Lutheran and has been since the Reformation. Ninety-one percent of all Danes belong to the Lutheran Evangelical Church of Denmark. One tour guide noted that Danes, who "are Lutheran if they are anything at all," go to church to be "hatched, matched, and dispatched." Women have been ordained as ministers since 1947.

The heavily taxed Danes even pay a church tax, and the last available statistics (1974) showed that 95% of the taxpayers did so, even in Copenhagen, where there are fewer churchgoers than in more rural areas. People of many other faiths will find houses of worship in Copenhagen, though one hotelier observed, "Only the Catholics look for a church."

FOLKLORE On June 23 (St. Hans Day), bonfires are burned around Denmark to celebrate the longest day and shortest night of the year. This tradition originally began to rid the land of witches and the disharmony they created.

2. FOOD & DRINK

The Danes relish their traditional buffet, *koldt bord* (the Swedish equivalent is the *smörgåsbord),* or "big cold table," as they refer to it, laden with herring, salmon, ham, roast beef, smoked turkey, pâté, cheeses, fruits, and desserts. A typical Danish buffet begins with fish, then meat, cheese, fruit, and dessert, and a new plate is provided for each course.

Herring, cod, and plaice are most often caught in the waters around Copenhagen, along with salmon, mackerel, eel, and deep-water shrimp.

A popular, filling dish called *biksemad* consists of meat, potatoes, and onions. Tasty, nonsweet breakfast rolls are called *grov birkes,* and the pastries are rich and wonderful, no matter which you select ("Napoleon's Hat" is delicious). No wonder "danish" has become the generic term for pastry.

No matter what you eat, however, you may wish to follow the Danish custom of drinking a cool pilsner beer and a shot of *aquavit*—a 90-proof potato-based schnapps. Aquavit comes in almost two dozen varieties.

Resign yourself to getting no free coffee refills; it's not the custom in Denmark.

3. RECOMMENDED BOOKS, FILMS & RECORDINGS

BOOKS

FICTION

Hans Christian Andersen (1805–75) is Denmark's most famous author, and his enduring fairy tales include *The Emperor's New Clothes, The Little Mermaid, The Princess and the Pea,* and *The Ugly Duckling,* available individually or in Andersen anthologies.

Baroness Karen Blixen, better known by her pseudonym, Isak Dinesen, another notable Danish author, was perhaps best known for *Out of Africa* (1938), which later became an award-winning film. Her first book, *Seven Gothic Tales* (1934), was written in English and first published in the United States. She was also author of *Winter Tales* (1942) and *Shadows in the Grass* (1960). An excellent biography is *Isak Dinesen—The Life of a Storyteller,* by Judith Thurman (St. Martin's Press, 1982).

Contemporary Danish writers who have been translated into English and whose works reveal the Danish experience and character include Nobel Prize–winner (1917) Henrik Pontoppidan, author of *The Promised Land,* the eight-volume *Lucky Peter,* and the five-volume *Kingdom of the Dead;* Martin Hansen, author or *Jonatan's Journey* (1941), *The Thornbush* (1946), *The Partridge* (1947), and (most notably) *The Liar* (1950); and Klaus Rifbjerg, author of poetry collections that include *Confrontation* (1960) and *Selected Poems* (1975) and the novel *Anna, I, Anna* (1969).

References that provide background information on modern Danish writers and their work include *A History of Scandinavian Literature,* by Sven H. Rosell (University of Minnesota Press), and the *International Dictionary of Twentieth Century Biography,* by Edward Vernoff and Renia Shore (New American Library).

PHILOSOPHY

Søren Kierkegaard (1813–55), the father of existentialism, deeply influenced the generations of thinkers who were to follow him with his philosophy based on "faith, knowledge, thought, and reality" as analyzed in his book *Either-Or.*

HISTORY

An Outline History of Denmark, by Helge Jacobsen, comes highly recommended; if it is not available in American bookstores, you'll find it in Copenhagen, along with the short, concise *Copenhagen—A Historical Guide,* by Torben Ejlersen (Host & Son), and *On a Tour to Nord Sjæaelland,* by Ole Schierbeck (Host & Son). Another historical resource is *A History of Scandinavia,* by T. K. Derry (University of Minnesota Press).

For a closer look at Scandinavia's Viking past, read *A History of the Vikings,* by Gwyn Jones (Oxford University Press), and *Vikings!,* by Magnus Magnusson (E. P. Dutton), illustrated with photographs.

CULTURE

Of Danish Ways, by sisters Ingeborg S. MacHaffie and Margaret A. Nielsen (Dillon Press), looks lovingly at customs and culture, along with history. Their book is an excellent choice for parents and children to read together.

If you are of Danish descent and want to delve into your background, *How to Find Your Family Roots,* by Timothy Field Bearch with Denise Demong (McGraw-Hill), is a good resource.

FILM

The Danish film industry produces about 20 films a year. Notable releases in recent years include Academy Award–winning *Babette's Feast* (1987), directed by Gabriel Axel; *Pelle the Conqueror* (1988), directed by Bille August and starring Max von Sydow; Academy Award–nominee *Waltzing Regitze* (released as *Memories of a Marriage,* 1989), directed by Kaspar Rostrup; and *Giselle* (1991), directed by Anne Rigitze Wivel, chronicling the evolution of a performance by the Royal Danish Ballet.

In 1952, Danny Kaye starred in *Hans Christian Andersen,* in which he popularized the song (and the expression) "Wonderful Copenhagen." If you're taking your children to Copenhagen, they'll love seeing Disney's animated version of *The Little Mermaid* (1989).

MUSIC

The beauty of the Danish countryside comes to life in the music of Carl Nielsen (1865–1931), most notably his cycle of six symphonies, available in CDs and on albums and cassettes.

Copenhagen is blessed with some of the world's best street musicians, who often sell cassettes of their music. Particularly outstanding are Jens Erik Raasted and Gernold Schonenberg who play primarily classical music on flute and guitar and, at last count, offer two fine cassettes of their work, "Musik på Strøget" ("Street Music in Copenhagen") and "Under Åben Himmel" ("Under the Open Sky").

Copenhagen is a city for the young, and some of the music they like best is written and performed by Kim Larsen and Eddie Skoller. Skoller, an American living in Copenhagen, sings in Danish and English; his music encompasses pop and jazz. Look for their CDs, cassettes, and albums in music stores.

FAMOUS COPENHAGENERS

Hans Christian Andersen (1805–75) One of the world's great tellers of fairy tales, author of *The Princess and the Pea, The Snow Queen, The Emperor's New Clothes,* and *The Little Mermaid,* among many others. He also wrote 30 plays, all of which have been forgotten.

Karen Blixen [Isak Dinesen] (1885–1962) An equally famous storyteller in another genre, she wrote *Seven Gothic Tales, Out of Africa,* and other books, and was twice nominated for the Nobel Prize for Literature.

Niels Bohr (1885–1962) Winner of the Nobel Prize for Physics in 1922 (his son Aage followed in his footsteps in 1975). His work marked the leap from atomic structure to quantum theory.

Victor Borge (1909–) Comedian, pianist, conductor, and humanitarian. Born Borge Rosenbaum and called the "Danish Noël Coward," he moved to the United States in 1940, when the Nazis invaded Denmark, and became a naturalized citizen in 1948. He was a guest for 54 consecutive weeks on the Kraft Music Hall.

Tycho Brahe (1546–1601) Said to be the greatest astronomer before the age of the telescope. Brahe quarreled with King Christian IV, left Copenhagen, and died in Prague.

Carl Th. Dreyer (1889–1968) Filmmaker, best known for the silent film classic *The Passion of Joan of Arc* (1928). Seven of his

14 films were shot in Denmark, including his last, *Gertrud* (1964). Other works include *Pages from Satan's Book* (1919), *The Parson's Widow* (1920), *Vampire* (1932), *Thou Shalt Honor Thy Wife* (1925), *Day of Wrath* (1943), and *The Word* (1955).

N. F. S. Grundtvig (1783–1872) Multitalented clergyman, historian, educator, writer, and composer of Danish hymns, he was also founder of the popular Folk High School movement in Denmark. He led a religious movement that has been described as "glad Christianity."

Martin Hansen (1909–55) Novelist, best known for *The Thornbush* (1946), *The Partridge* (1947), and particularly *The Liar* (1950), which was written in diary form.

Ludvig Holberg (1684–1754) Comedy writer, called the Danish Molière, and considered the father of Danish theater.

Arne Jacobsen (1902–71) The best known modern Danish architect, designer of the SAS Royal Hotel, Copenhagen's first "skyscraper," in 1960. He also designed furniture and household items.

Jens Peter Jacobsen (1847–85) Poet and novelist who began writing after contracting tuberculosis in 1873. Author of *Fru Marie Grubbe* (1876), a psychological study; *Niels Lynne* (1880), about an atheist in the modern world; and *Mogens and Other Stories* (1882). Before becoming a writer, he was a scientist, credited with introducing Darwin's theories to Denmark.

Georg Jensen (1866–1935) Trained as a sculptor but famous as a silversmith and founder in 1904 of the internationally known company bearing his name.

Søren Kierkegaard (1813–55) The author of works on philosophy and religion, and the father of existentialism. He produced a "unique body of work that resembles nothing else in the whole of world literature" that greatly influenced 20th-century thought.

Peter Martins (1946–) Dancer (a tall one, at 6′, 1″), choreographer, currently creative director of New York City Ballet. At age 20, he was a principal with the Royal Danish Ballet in Copenhagen, where he received his initial training.

Carl Nielsen (1865–1931) Composer of two operas, *Saul and David* and *Masquerade,* six symphonies, and three concerti. His Opus 1 *Suite for Strings* was performed at Tivoli in 1888 and continues to be featured in concert programs.

Hans Christian Ørsted (1777–1851) Physicist, chemist, and teacher who made a discovery in 1820 that led to the theory of electromagnetism.

Henrik Pontoppidan (1857–1943) Cowinner of the Nobel Prize for Literature in 1917 for his "authentic description of present-day life in Denmark." Major works include *The Promised*

Land, eight-volume *Lucky Peter,* and five-volume *The Kingdom of the Dead.*

Klaus Rifbjerg (1931–) Novelist and poet, best known for *Confrontation* (1960) the third collection of his poetry, and for the novel *Anna, I, Anna* 1969). His *Selected Poems* was translated into English in 1975.

Bertel Thorvaldsen (1768–1844) Denmark's best known classical sculptor. He lived and worked in Rome for 41 years, often for the nobility; he returned to his native land in 1838. He bequeathed his collection to Copenhagen, and it may be seen at the Thorvaldsen Museum

CHAPTER 2

PLANNING A TRIP TO COPENHAGEN

After deciding where to go, most people ask these questions: How do I get there? What will it cost? Where do I find information? This chapter addresses these questions and other important issues that you should consider even before you arrive in Copenhagen, such as whether or not to purchase travel insurance, where the best bargains are, and how to stick to a budget.

1. INFORMATION, ENTRY REQUIREMENTS & MONEY

SOURCES OF INFORMATION

IN THE U.S.A. & CANADA

General information on Copenhagen and Denmark may be obtained from the following tourist offices:

Chicago: Scandinavian Tourist Office, 150 North Michigan Avenue, Chicago, IL 60601 (tel. 312/726-1120).

New York: Danish Tourist Board, 655 Third Avenue, 18th floor, New York, NY 10017 (tel. 212/949-2333).

Los Angeles: Danish Tourist Board, 8929 Wilshire Boulevard, Los Angeles, CA 90211 (tel. 213/657-4808).

Toronto: Danish Tourist Board, P.O. Box 115, Station N, Toronto, ON M8V 3S4, Canada (tel. 416/823-9620).

IMPRESSIONS

Between the Baltic Sea and the North Sea lies an old swan's nest. It is called "Denmark."
—HANS CHRISTIAN ANDERSEN

IN COPENHAGEN

There are two helpful sources of information in Copenhagen:

The **Danish Tourist Board,** H. C. Andersens Boulevard 22 (tel. 33/11-13-25), provides hostel and hotel accommodations information and can answer specific questions about Copenhagen and the rest of Denmark.

Use-It, at Huset, Rådhusstræde 13, second floor (tel. 33/15-65-18), has information specifically geared to youth and budget travel (see "Tourist Information," in Chapter 3).

ENTRY REQUIREMENTS

DOCUMENTS

Citizens of the United States, Canada, New Zealand, and Australia need only a valid passport to enter Denmark. Members of the European Economic Community, which includes Great Britain and Ireland, need only a valid EEC passport.

CUSTOMS

Visitors 17 years and older may bring in duty free one liter of alcohol (always an appreciated gift) or 10 liters (about 30 bottles) of beer, although that's like bringing coal to Newcastle. Visitors may also bring in up to 200 cigarettes.

Alcohol and tobacco is sold duty free in restricted quantities on ships and ferries making short Scandinavian crossings. Each adult is allowed 20 cigarettes, for example.

You pay no duty on personal items such as cameras, musical instruments (or on money made playing them on Strøget!), and laptop computers, as long as you take them with you when you leave.

Dogs and cats may be imported from the United States with a veterinarian's certificate issued on a special form; if Tabby or Bowser is coming from Great Britain, Ireland, New Zealand, Australia, or Japan, no certificate is required.

Remember that Customs regulations are subject to change, and may do so quite drastically with the opening of the European borders in 1992. To double-check the above or get more information, contact the Danish consulate nearest you.

MONEY

The Danish currency is the **krone** (crown), or **kroner (Kr)** in its plural form, made up of 100 **ore.** Banknotes are issued in 20, 50, 100, 500, and 1,000 kroner. Coins come in 25 and 50 ore, and 1, 5, 10, and 20 kroner. Denmark's monetary system is undergoing changes now through 1993, with new coins being introduced; old coins and banknotes may be exchanged at banks.

At this writing, $1 = approximately 5.70 kroner (or 1 krone = 18.5¢), and this rate of exchange (*x* Kr ÷ 5.7 = $*y*) was used to calculate the dollar values given throughout this book (rounded to the nearest nickel). This rate fluctuates from time to time and may not be the same when you travel to Denmark, so please use the following table only as a guide.

DANISH KRONER & U.S. DOLLAR EQUIVALENTS

Kr	U.S.	Kr	U.S.
1	.18	100	17.54
2	.35	125	21.93
3	.53	150	26.32
4	.70	175	30.70
5	.88	200	35.09
6	1.05	225	39.47
7	1.23	250	43.86
8	1.40	275	48.25
9	1.58	300	52.63
10	1.75	325	57.02
15	2.63	350	61.40
20	3.51	375	65.79
25	4.39	400	70.18
50	8.77	500	87.72

TRAVELER'S CHECKS & CREDIT CARDS

Internationally recognized traveler's checks and credit cards are accepted throughout Denmark. Banks will also cash *Eurocheques,* as will shops when they are drawn in Danish currency.

WHAT THINGS COST IN COPENHAGEN	U.S. $
Taxi from Central Station to Amalienborg Castle	$8.80
S-tog from Central Station to outlying neighborhood	$1.40

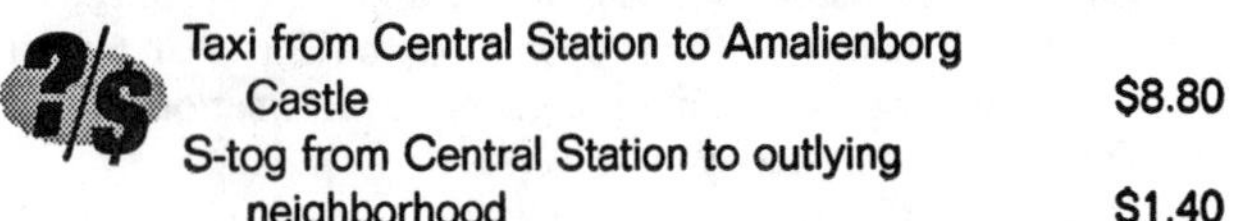

	U.S. $
Local telephone call	.09
Double room at the SAS Royal Hotel (deluxe)	340.00
Double room, without bath, at the Saga Hotel (moderate)	89.50
Double room at the 9 Små Hjem (budget, summer only)	38.60
Lunch for one at Sporvejen (moderate)	8.60
Lunch for one at Klaptræct (budget)	6.10
Dinner for one, without wine, at Els (deluxe)	37.55
Dinner for one, without wine, at Pasta Basta (moderate)	12.10
Dinner for one, without wine, at Shezan (budget)	9.25
Pint of beer or glass of wine	3.70
Cup of coffee in a café	2.45
Roll of ASA 100 color, 36 exposures	11.05
Admission to Tivoli	4.90
Admission to the Ny Carlsberg Glyptotek Museum	2.65
Movie ticket	10.50
Theater ticket at the Royal Theater	7.00

2. WHEN TO GO — CLIMATE, HOLIDAYS & EVENTS

CLIMATE

Copenhagen is at its best from the end of April to the beginning of September, when days are long, Tivoli is open, and sidewalk cafés

IMPRESSIONS

Copenhageners are generally easygoing and informal . . . more open and outspoken than most other Danes.

—Collier's Encyclopedia

buzz long into the night. Of course, other seasons have their advantages, including less precipitation, fewer tourists, and, in general, lower prices. Christmas in Copenhagen is especially memorable.

Copenhagen's Average Temperatures & Rainfall

	Jan	Feb	Mar	Apr	May	June	July	Aug	Sept	Oct	Nov	Dec
Temp (°F)	32	31	36	44	53	60	64	63	57	49	42	37
Rainfall "	1.9	1.5	1.2	1.5	1.7	1.8	2.8	2.6	2.4	2.3	1.9	1.9

HOLIDAYS

Copenhagen celebrates these public holidays: New Year's Day (Jan 1), Maundy Thursday (the Thursday before Good Friday), Good Friday, Easter Sunday, Easter Monday, Ascension Day, Whitmonday, Constitution Day (June 5, from noon), Christmas Eve, Christmas Day, Boxing Day (Dec 26).

COPENHAGEN CALENDAR OF EVENTS

Most of the following special events occur in Copenhagen. However, a few of particular note have been included because they warrant an excursion if you're so inclined.

APRIL

- ☐ The **Queen's birthday** falls on April 16, cause for great celebration among her devoted subjects. The Life Guard don red uniforms, and the royal family waves from the balcony of their residence at Amalienborg Square at noon.
- ☐ ✪ **Tivoli** opens and will remain so until mid-September, filling Copenhagen days and nights with its unique, infectious liveliness.

MAY

- ☐ The **Copenhagen Carnival** is held the end of May, with a raucous Mardi Gras party, complete with costumes and sambas.
- ☐ Another highlight is the annual **Wonderful Copenhagen Marathon;** if you'd like to run in it, contact marathon headquarters at Ndr. Fasanvej 152, DK-2000, Frederiksberg, Denmark (tel. 31/34-14-00).

☐ **May Day** is celebrated informally in Fælledparken by Copenhageners who are thrilled to bid winter good-bye.

JUNE

☐ ✪ **Free park concerts,** most notably in Fælledparken, begin in June and continue throughout the summer.

☐ The **Skagen Festival,** held the last few days in June, is a major folk event filled with folk songs and folk rock. Skagen, a seaside resort, is the most northern town on the Jutland peninsula.

JULY

☐ ✪ The **Copenhagen Jazz Festival** is held during the first part of July, and the **Copenhagen Summer Festival,** which highlights classical music, lasts for 3½ weeks in July.

☐ Believe it or not, America's **Fourth of July** (Independence Day) has been celebrated in Denmark since 1912 in the Rebild Hills in Jutland. Besides entertainment, speeches are delivered by notable Danes and Americans (Garrison Keillor in 1991).

SEPTEMBER

☐ The **Aarhus International Festival,** usually the second week of September, presents Copenhagen's most comprehensive program of concerts, sports, theater, and exhibitions. There's an old-fashioned fair in the Old Town open-air museum and a medieval one at Moesgaard Prehistoric Museum. Aarhus is 180 miles (288km) from Copenhagen, on the Jutland peninsula.

3. INSURANCE

Before leaving home, check to see if your health and property coverage extends to Europe. If it doesn't, or the coverage is inadequate, consider purchasing short-term travel insurance that will cover medical and other emergencies.

Also check your homeowner's or renter's insurance for coverage for off-premises theft. Again, if you need more coverage, consider a short-term policy.

If you are traveling as part of a tour or have prepaid many of your vacation expenses, you may also want to purchase insurance that covers you if you have to cancel for any reason.

Your best bet may be to purchase a comprehensive travel policy that covers all catastrophes, big and small—trip cancellation, health, emergency assistance, and lost luggage. A travel agent may sell you a policy (the price is small), or contact the following companies for more information:

Tele-Trip (Mutual of Omaha), 3201 Farnam Street, Omaha, NE 68131 (tel. toll free 800/228-9792).

Travel Guard International, 45 Clark Street, Stevens Point, WI 54482 (tel. toll free 800/826-1300).

Travel Insurance Pak, Traveler's Insurance Co., One Tower Square, 15NB, Hartford, CT 06183-5040 (tel. toll free 800/243-3174).

For travel assistance, which bails you out with a loan of money in case of a serious midtrip medical emergency, contact:

Access America, 600 Third Avenue, New York, NY 10016 (tel. toll free 800/284-8300).

HealthCare Abroad (Medex), 243 Church Street NW, Suite 100D, Vienna, VA 22180 (tel. toll free 800/237-6615).

4. WHAT TO PACK

Less is liberating. Never bring more luggage than you can carry. One bag (or backpack) is ideal. The bare-bones packing rule on garments is two: Wash one, wear one.

CLOTHING

Summers are cooler in Copenhagen than in most of Europe, so bring a sweater; a raincoat with removable lining is always practical in spring or autumn, and a coat—and long johns—in winter, when temperatures hover around the freezing point. Year round, slacks are more popular here than jeans.

If you are traveling with only a change or two of clothes, bring along some accessories to add a little diversity to your wardrobe: jewelry, a favorite hat, scarves, a vest, or tie.

In winter, pack boots suitable for walking in snow. Comfortable walking shoes are essential; if you buy new ones for the trip, be sure to break them in before you arrive.

Avoid dry-clean-only apparel because the cost in Copenhagen is the equivalent of a good meal. Simple Laundromats are expensive enough, so choose articles that do not soil easily (or noticeably).

OTHER ITEMS

Bring your favorite brand of toiletries in sample sizes, and pack extra if you think you'll need them and they're not too heavy (tampons and condoms come to mind).

Bring a wash cloth if you're in the habit of using one; hotels don't provide them.

Also pack your converter and adapter plugs, travel alarm, a small flashlight, copies of your passport and other valuable documents and means of identification, prescriptions for drugs or eyeglasses, a Swiss Army knife, a collapsible umbrella, a sewing kit, and a sleep sheet if you plan to stay in hostels (they won't accept your sleeping bag).

5. TIPS FOR TRAVELERS

FOR THE DISABLED

Mobility International, P.O. Box 3551, Eugene, OR 97403 (tel. 503/343-1284), can provide information on travel, educational exchanges, and work camps.

The **Travel Information Service** of Moss Rehabilitation Hospital, 1200 West Tabor Road, Philadelphia, PA 19141-3099 (tel. 215/456-9600), a center for treatment for the physically handicapped, has information on accessible hotels, restaurants, and attractions in Denmark, much of it supplied from firsthand reports.

Check your bookstore for *Access to the World: A Travel Guide for the Handicapped,* an informative 220-page book by Louise Weiss (Henry Holt).

FOR SENIORS

In Copenhagen, people over age 67 are entitled to half-price tickets at the Royal Theater, reduced admission to some museums, and discounts on ferries to Sweden. Keep that ID handy.

If you aren't already a member, consider joining the **American Association of Retired Persons (AARP),** 1909 K Street NW, Washington, DC 20049 (tel. 202/872-4700), which has a Purchase Privilege Program with discounts on lodging and car rentals abroad.

FOR SINGLE TRAVELERS

Take advantage of meeting Danish members of **Servas** or **Friends Overseas,** organizations that encourage peoples of different cultures to get together (see "Home Stays or Visits," below). As far as lodging is concerned, remember that some private homes (as opposed to hotels) charge a **per-person room rate** rather than a separate double and single (higher) rate. This works out in the single person's favor. In Copenhagen, people are naturally friendly, and it's easy to strike up conversations with them.

FOR FAMILIES

A valuable source of information for families is *Family Travel Times,* a newsletter published 10 times a year by Travel with Your Children (TWYCH), 80 Eighth Avenue, New York, NY 10011 (tel. 212/206-0688); subscribers have access to a call-in service that will answer their questions on travel in specific countries.

Copenhagen welcomes families to its parks, Tivoli, Strøget, and free outdoor entertainment and activities in summer. Museums offer reduced admission for children. On public transportation, children between the ages of 5 and 12 pay half price; younger kids travel for free.

If you're traveling with teenagers, they'll be forever grateful that you've brought them to Copenhagen, as the city is loved by young people from all around the world, and rightfully so.

FOR STUDENTS & YOUTH

To enjoy special discounts while visiting the city, flash the **International Student Identity Card (ISIC)** or, if you're student age but not a student, the **International Youth Identity Card.** Both carry basic accident and sickness insurance coverage, have a hotline for medical, legal, and financial emergencies, and are available for $14 from the **Council on International Educational Exchange (CIEE),** 205 East 42nd Street, New York, NY 10017 (tel. 212/661-1450).

6. ALTERNATIVE/ADVENTURE TRAVEL

EDUCATIONAL/STUDY TRAVEL

Denmark offers the unique "folk high school," an adult residential college with courses of two or more weeks' duration taught in English. No exams, no certificates when you enter or depart—just learning for the sake of learning. Contact **Den Internationale Højskole (International Peoples' College),** Montebello Allé 1, DK-3000 Helsingør, Denmark (tel. 49/21-33-61).

The **Institute of International Education (IIE),** 809 United Nations Plaza, New York, NY 10017 (tel. 212/883-8200), and the **Council on International Educational Exchange** (address and phone under "For Students and Youth," above) provide free booklets and also sell books about study (and teaching) abroad.

Those 50 and older may partake of courses in Copenhagen offered by **Interhostel,** University of New Hampshire, 6 Garrison Avenue, Durham, NH 03824 (tel. toll free 800/733-9753 or 603/862-1147), and, for people 60 and older, **Elderhostel,** 75 Federal Street, Boston, MA 02110-1941 (tel. 617/426-7788).

HOME STAYS OR VISITS

Anyone would be enriched by a one-to-one exchange with a friendly Copenhagener. To set up a visit, be it for afternoon tea or a shared excursion or a home stay, consider joining **Friends Overseas,** 68-04 Dartmouth Street, Forest Hills, NY 11375 (no phone). The organization has a successful American-Scandinavian People-to-People Program, and travelers pay $25 per visit to participate. For more information, send a stamped, business-size envelope to the above address.

Another organization, **Servas,** was founded in Denmark in 1949 to promote peace and understanding by getting people of different cultures together. It has 69 hosts in Copenhagen, 250 in Denmark. For more information, contact Servas at 11 John Street, Suite 706, New York, NY 10038-4009 (tel. 212/267-0252); the yearly membership is $45, with a $15 refundable deposit for host lists.

The **International Visitors Information Service,** 733 15th Street NW, Suite 300, Washington, DC 20005 (tel. 202/783-6540), lists organizations in 35 countries, including Denmark, in its *Meet the People* directory ($6.50).

WORK CAMPS

Participants in work camps arrange and pay for their own transportation but work in exchange for room and board and the chance to perform socially significant tasks. Volunteers generally spend 2 to 3 weeks at a camp, and work a 5-day, 30-hour week in groups of 5 to 30 people. The minimum age to participate is 16 or 18; there is no maximum age. Most work camps take place from June through September.

IMPRESSIONS

Just living is not enough! One must have sunshine, freedom, and a little flower.

—Hans Christian Andersen

To inquire about work camps in the Copenhagen environs or in other parts of Denmark, contact **Volunteers for Peace International Workcamps,** 43 Tiffany Road, Belmont, VT 05730 (tel. 802/259-2759); **SCI International Voluntary Service,** c/o Innisfree Village, Route 2, Box 506, Crozet, VA 22932 (tel. 804/823-1826); and the **Council on International Educational Exchange,** 205 East 42nd Street, New York, NY 10017 (tel. 212/661-1414).

APARTMENT RENTALS

If you plan to stay in Copenhagen a month or longer, an apartment rental may be an economical and comfortable choice for lodging. **Use-It,** Copenhagen's helpful alternative information center, has notebooks filled with apartment rentals giving a description, share or sublet information, and the cost. There's a table where you may sit and leaf through the offerings. Use-It is on the second floor of Huset (The House), Rådhusstræde 13 (tel. 33/15-65-18), not far from the main pedestrian street, Strøget.

HOME EXCHANGES

If you'd like to swap your house or apartment for one in Copenhagen and live like a true Copenhagener, contact the **Vacation Exchange Club,** Box 820, Haleiwa, HI 96712 (tel. toll free 800/638-3841). The club's directory of more than 10,000 listings is published twice a year.

7. GETTING THERE

BY PLANE

THE MAJOR AIRLINES

Scandinavian Airlines is the national carrier serving Denmark, Sweden, and Norway, with 5 daily flights in summer from Los Angeles, Seattle, and Chicago; 7 from New York; and 3 from Toronto. Off-season (mid-September through April), there are slightly fewer flights per day.

Other airlines offering direct flights between North American gateways and Copenhagen include TWA and Delta (from Atlanta).

Airlines flying to Copenhagen via another destination include **Finnair** (via Helsinki), **Icelandair** (via Reykjavik), and **KLM** (via Amsterdam). For flights arriving from gateways outside North America, see "Arriving by Plane" in Chapter 3.

Flights arrive at Copenhagen Airport, only 6 miles south of the downtown area.

BEST-FOR-THE-BUDGET FARES

With an eye toward frugality, consider some alternative ways of getting to Copenhagen by air. Retail discount ticket agencies, or **bucket shops,** offer reductions of 20% to 30%, usually advertised in the travel sections of newspapers. Postage-stamp-size ads simply list major European cities with a fare opposite each one. The tickets are restrictive, nontransferable, and nonrefundable except directly from the bucket shop.

Leading retail bucket shops selling air transportation to Copenhagen include **Access International Inc.,** 101 West 31st Street, Suite 1104, New York, NY 10001 (tel. toll free 800/827-3633 or 212/465-0707 in New York); **Maharajah Travels, Inc.,** 395 Fifth Avenue, New York, NY 10016 (tel. toll free 800/223-6882 or 212/213-2020 in New York); **Sunline Express Holidays, Inc.,** 607 Market Street, San Francisco, CA 94105 (tel. toll free 800/877-2111 or 415/541-7800); and **Euro-Asia, Inc.,** 4203 East Indian School Road, Suite 210, Phoenix, AZ 85018 (tel. toll free 800/525-3876 or 602/955-2742), which also offers discounted fares through travel agents.

Some **"budget" airlines** have a reputation for consistently low fares—though, to be honest, in the last few years, they have not been significantly lower than other carriers' fares. Still, be sure to check **Tower Air** (tel. toll free 800/221-2500) or **Icelandair** (tel. toll free 800/223-5500). The latter flies to Luxembourg, and from there you can get to Copenhagen by train.

Also consider **charter flights** to Copenhagen. Drop by a travel agency and ask to see their most recent copy of the monthly magazine of the air chartering industry, *Jax Fax,* to ferret out dates, departure cities, and prices for charter transportation between North America and Europe. The closest you may be able to get is Amsterdam or Frankfurt and then take the train.

If you're traveling alone and light—meaning one or two carry-on bags only—consider going as a **courier.** You get a greatly reduced fare and the courier company gets your checked-baggage space for its time-sensitive packages. The courier company only offers one seat a day, so if two of you are traveling together, try to arrange departures on two consecutive days. For more information, check the *Yellow Pages* of your telephone directory for courier services in your area, or contact **Now Voyager Freelance Couriers,** 74 Varick Street, Suite 307, New York, NY 10013 (tel. 212/431-1616).

REGULAR AIRFARES

If you can't find a bucket-shop, charter, or courier flight to save on airfare, look at what's being offered by the carriers that fly to Copenhagen on a regular basis, such as **SAS, Finnair, Icelandair,** and **American.** They are sure to have ads in the travel section of your local newspaper.

If time is on your side, take advantage of significantly reduced **early fares,** available to those who can commit two or three months in advance to a particular flight and can stay a minimum 7 days, a maximum 30 days. For example, in 1991 SAS offered an early-bird fare of $598 round trip from New York to Copenhagen in summer, $498 for flights made off-season (add an additional $100 for flights from Chicago and Minneapolis, $200 from the West Coast) for anyone who could commit to a date by April 8. Keep in mind that an "early fare" does not refer to the time the plane departs but to the time of the booking.

Advance-purchase fares are also economical, though not as much as the early-bird specials. To get them, you usually have to purchase the ticket 14 to 30 days before departure and stay in Europe at least a week but no longer than three weeks. Some advance-purchase fares don't even have the two-week lead time; I've seen one-day advance purchase fares advertised. The fares are generally lower for midweek than weekend flights. If you are a student or a senior citizen, always ask if a special discount applies to you.

If advance-purchase fares aren't available, then you have to resort to regularly scheduled flights, and they offer three fare possibilities: **coach,** with the most economical, and also the most cramped, seats; costlier **business class,** with more amenities and more legroom (ask about an upgrade from coach; it may be less than you think and worth it for the lengthy transatlantic flight); and **first class,** the most expensive.

If you have to leave at a moment's notice, you may have to fly **standby,** taking whatever seat is available, be it coach, business class, or first class. Flying standby is not comparable to standing on a half-price ticket line for whatever seat is available at the theater. No discount here.

If you have to fly to or from Europe because of the death of a

FROMMER'S SMART TRAVELER: AIRFARES

- The farther ahead you plan—and book your flight—the better you fair on the fare. The airline is happy to have your money and will compensate you for your early commitment.
- If you plan to stay only a week (or less), look into specific land-air packages, which represent big savings—the equivalent of having hotel and breakfast thrown in for free.
- Comparison-shop all the airlines that fly to Copenhagen. Also consider flights to nearby cities, such as Amsterdam or Berlin, if the price is right. Fares to the three Scandinavian capitals are usually comparable.
- Inquire about early-bird, advance-purchase, and other discount fares, even if you have not seen them advertised.
- Keep calling airlines to check fares. Availability of inexpensive seats changes daily, depending on the airline, and as the departure dates draws near, some airlines sell more seats at lower prices.
- Ask about senior or student discounts (SAS offers both).
- Consider flying in a shoulder (not quite peak) season, such as late September, October, late April, or early May, when fares are lower and the weather pleasant. Tivoli opens the last week of April and doesn't close until mid-September, so you can enjoy both a discount airline ticket and this unique Copenhagen phenomenon.
- The opening of borders in the European community in 1992 may open the way for lowered fares within individual countries and within Europe itself. If you're pressed for time and have to fly from one city to another in Denmark, Scandinavia, or Europe, it's going to be more economical now than ever before.

family member, some airlines offer a **bereavement fare.** It's not available through SAS, however.

BY TRAIN

Trains arrive frequently at Copenhagen's centrally located Central Station from other countries and other parts of Denmark. There is an S-tog (commuter train) stop here, as well, for connections to outlying areas of the city.

The most economical way to travel to Copenhagen by train usually is via a **ScanRail pass,** valid for travel in Denmark, Sweden, and Norway. The pass costs $170 first class, $139 second class, for any 4 days of rail travel in a 15-day period.

If you will be arriving in Copenhagen from a part of Europe other than Scandinavia, consider purchasing a **Eurailpass,** which costs $230 for 5 days of travel within a 15-day period. Both ScanRail and Eurail passes are available for longer periods than those mentioned above. They both must be purchased in the United States.

In many cases, the cost of either pass is less than you would pay for individual tickets to get from place to place.

For more information on ScanRail or Eurail passes, contact **Rail Europe,** Information Department, 230 Westchester Avenue, White Plains, NY 10604 (tel. 914/682-5172 if you are in New York, New Jersey, Connecticut, or Canada; toll free 800/345-1990 in the rest of the United States).

BY BUS

To tell the truth, people rarely arrive in Copenhagen by bus. They take a train or plane. There are bus connections into Central Station from Malmö, Lund, and Ystad, Sweden, and into Copenhagen Airport from Malmö and Halmstad (via Angelholm Airport), Sweden. In Denmark, long-distance bus service is available between Copenhagen and Aalborg, Hanstholm, Aarhus, Odense, and Nykøbing Falster. Most of the buses you'll see, or most likely use, provide a link between small Danish towns that have no rail or air service.

BY CAR

Copenhagen is 180 miles (288km) from Hamburg, 400 miles (640km) from Stockholm, and 405 miles (648km) from Oslo.

The only direct land link to Denmark from other parts of Europe is via Flensburg in Germany, but you eventually have to cross water to get to North Zealand and Copenhagen. There is car ferry service between Malmö and Helsingborg, Sweden, and Copenhagen and Helsingør, respectively, as well as between Limhamn, Sweden, and Dragør, just south of Copenhagen Airport. The rates are reasonable.

In Denmark, the speed limit is 100km (62 miles) per hour on motorways, 80km (50 miles) per hour on smaller roads, and 50km (25 miles) per hour in populated areas. Speed limits are given in kilometers, and one is equal to about ⅔ mile.

If you plan to drive in Denmark (anywhere in Europe), you will need an **international driver's license,** available for $10 through any branch of **American Automobile Association (AAA).** If you are a member of AAA, find out which auto associations in Denmark have a reciprocal agreement with it (there are several). AAA headquarters is at 1000 AAA Drive, Heathrow, FL 32746-5063 (tel. 407/444-8000).

BY FERRY

Even before the days of Bishop Absalon, there has been a ferry route linking Copenhagen and Sweden. Today a high-speed craft zips between **Malmö** and Copenhagen in 45 minutes; passengers may enjoy a meal and duty-free drinks on board (in fact, for some Swedes and Danes, it's a less expensive night out than going out at home).

There is also a ferry connection between **Helsingborg,** Sweden, and Helsingør, in Hamlet country half an hour north of Copenhagen.

BY SHIP

The gateway to Scandinavia, Copenhagen is home port to 85% of all ships cruising the Baltic Sea (at last count that was 110). Among the cruise lines docking at Langelinie are **Bergen Line,** who represents **Silja Line** (tel. 212/986-2711, toll free 800/323-7436), and **Scandinavian Seaways** (tel. toll free 800/533-3755 in the U.S. and Canada). For a more extensive list, contact a travel agent or the Danish Tourist Board.

PACKAGE TOURS

Fly-drive holidays and Scandinavian vacation packages are available from September to May 15 from **SAS Viking Vacations** (tel. toll free 800/344-9099; fax 212/779-8944). City package tours of one to 30 days are offered year round by **Scantours** (tel. toll free 800/223-SCAN; fax 213/395-2013) and **SuperCities** (tel. toll free 800/888-8685), and from April through October (three or six days only) by **American Express Travel** (tel. 404/368-5100; fax 404/368-5184).

In Copenhagen, **Scandinavian Express,** Antonigade 4, fourth

---

IMPRESSIONS

The Sound is so packed with herrings that the boats stand on the fish and the oars can scarcely drive the craft through the waters.

—SAXO GRAMMATICUS, DANISH HISTORIAN 13TH CENTURY

floor (tel. 33/13-40-13; fax 33/93-19-61), offers a budget tour of the Scandinavian capitals (Copenhagen, Oslo, and Stockholm). The company is represented in the United States by **Scanworld,** 12444 Ventura Boulevard, Studio City, CA 91604 (tel. toll free 800/622-5355; Canadians call collect 818/506-4114).

8. ENJOYING COPENHAGEN ON A BUDGET

THE $50-A-DAY BUDGET

First the bad news: Scandinavian countries are some of the most expensive in Europe. Now the good news: Denmark is the least expensive of all of them to visit. If you're coming from Stockholm or Oslo, Copenhagen will seem like the bargain center of the universe. If you stay in youth hostels or private homes, you can spend $50 a day or less. If you insist on staying at a hotel, you'll have to budget more.

For two people traveling together, which is the most economical way to do it, figure *each* person will spend roughly $40 a day on a hotel room with bath (if you opt for a private home, figure about $23, and for a hostel $10 to $17 a day). Factor in another $20 for meals; that's giving you a minuscule allowance for alcohol, but plenty for delicious danish pastries and one light meal and one substantial one. Don't forget, a filling Danish breakfast is included in the price of most hotel rooms.

What you spend on activities, entertainment, and transportation is not figured into the dollar-a-day amount here. Fortunately, the layout of Copenhagen encourages walking, which keeps transportation expenses low; the Copenhagen Card (see Chapter 3), truly a good deal, covers bus and train fares, plus admission to Tivoli and lots of museums; and some of the best entertainment in town—that found along Strøget—is free as the air you breathe.

To stick to your $50 a day (or less) goal, be creative—and selective. The tips below will help.

SAVING MONEY ON ACCOMMODATIONS

Youth hostels are cheapest, but in Copenhagen, they are not located right downtown (a pseudo-dorm provides temporary lodging in summer only). Your next bet is lodging in private homes, which affords more privacy than a hostel with the benefit of your getting to know your Danish host. Hotels around the train station are less expensive than others in the city and centrally located; rates at some of them drop off-season, from mid-September to April.

If you like interacting with local folks and don't mind giving up some touring time for chatting, home stays are a wonderful alternative to staying in hotels or other lodging. While you don't pay anything, you must have the courtesy to keep respectable hours, be a quiet, thoughtful guest, arrive when you say you will, and spend time sharing bits and pieces of your life with your host, who will do the same with you.

SAVING MONEY ON MEALS

Plan on spending at least $10 on one hearty meal a day, and eat smaller ones and/or snacks throughout the day to tide you over. You can cook in one of the city's three hostels and in some private homes (see individual listings). Buy fresh fruit, which is both satisfying and healthful for you. Make lunch rather than dinner your main meal of the day. If you're staying in a hotel, choose one that includes breakfast in the room rate; the breakfast buffets are enormous.

SAVING MONEY ON SIGHTSEEING & OTHER ENTERTAINMENT

This is easy in Copenhagen, where part of the fun is simply ambling along the many pedestrian thoroughfares, people watching, and soaking up the atmosphere and architecture. The benefits are twofold: It's free and good exercise. Some of the best entertainment in Europe is right on Strøget, the mile-long pedestrian street. If you want to throw a few coins into the performer's instrument case or hat, or buy a cassette from him or her, that's up to you. Major attractions can easily be visited without benefit of a tour; some require a train or bus ride, though. There are free concerts in the city's parks in summer, and the Copenhagen Card, good for one, two, or three days, provides big savings year round (see Chapter 3).

SAVING MONEY ON SHOPPING

Window shopping along Strøget is absolutely free. To actually drop a little cash, you'd best explore the side streets. If you buy a lot, save the receipts and get the VAT (the goods and services tax) back when you leave the country. My favorite place to shop is the grocery stores, where candles and napkins are so inexpensive and a wonderful souvenir of the city. If the shops in Copenhagen don't convince you to part with some money, those at Copenhagen Airport will. Allow time to browse its 30 shops before departing; you're bound to unearth a bargain or two.

SAVING MONEY ON SERVICES & OTHER TRANSACTIONS

MONEY EXCHANGE

You'll get a better exchange rate if you change traveler's checks at banks rather than at hotels or in shops. If you use your credit card, *you'll receive the going exchange rate when the bill arrives at the headquarters of your credit card company,* be it two weeks or two months after you made the purchase. (This does not work in your favor if the dollar is growing weaker by the day.)

PHONE CALLS HOME

The least expensive way to place phone calls from abroad is by pay phone, never the phone in your hotel room. Call collect or use your calling card or credit card (which some readers claim is the best bargain of all).

TIPPING

Tipping is the exception—never the rule—in Copenhagen; a tip is included in restaurant bills and taxi fares (you can round it up if you feel like it).

CHAPTER 3

GETTING TO KNOW COPENHAGEN

Copenhagen is the kind of place where you feel at home right away. It's cosmopolitan but with a bohemian flair, ages-old yet young and sassy, and appealing to people of all ages for all reasons. This chapter will help you get your bearings, and you'll be exploring on your own in no time.

1. ORIENTATION

ARRIVING

BY PLANE

AIRPORT Is it a top-of-the-line department store or is it an airport? It's both! Copenhagen Airport, originally called Kastrup (tel. 31/50-93-33), located only 6 miles from the city center, could be the fanciest place to land in Europe. The bank in the Arrival Hall offers reasonable exchange rates; it's open daily from 6:30am to 10pm. Public telephones accept a number of foreign coins—including American quarters. There's also a café, a small market, rental-car counters including Avis, Budget, Hertz, and Pitzner (a Danish company that claims to have the lowest rates), and courtesy baggage carts.

In the adjacent Departure Hall, the Left Luggage Office (tel. 31/50-88-89), open daily from 6:30am to 11pm, charges 20 Kr ($3.50) per bag per day, 30 Kr ($5.25) for bikes and skis. Opposite the Luggage Office is a post office (enter through the red door), open weekdays from 9am to 5:30pm, Saturday until noon.

AIRLINES Copenhagen is served by a number of airlines, most frequently by **SAS,** which has about 200 international flights into Copenhagen Airport daily. Also calling on a regular basis are Aer Lingus, Air France, Alitalia, British Airways, Canadian Airlines,

Icelandair, Finnair, Japan Airlines, KLM, Northwest, Olympic Airways, Pan American, Singapore Airlines, TAP Air Portugal, Quantas, TWA, and Varig. These airlines all have offices in Copenhagen.

GETTING TO & FROM THE AIRPORT The **SAS Airport Bus** (tel. 32/52-00-66) departs every 15 minutes and runs between the main terminal and Copenhagen's Central Station; the trip takes about 25 minutes and costs 26 Kr ($4.55); children under 12 free. There are usually several SAS buses parked out front, so be sure you're on the one going downtown.

City bus no. 32 also makes the run between the airport and the city center (Town Hall Square); buses depart every 20 minutes or so and the 45-minute journey costs just 9 Kr ($1.60).

BY TRAIN

Central Station is relatively easy to negotiate. The **train information and room service windows** and lockers are located in the center of the station, while shops, banks, ticket windows, and platform entrances are located around the perimeter. The information window is open daily from 9am to 7pm; the hotel reservations window, from 9am to midnight May through August and 9am to 10pm September through April.

The **luggage-storage office** is open daily from 6:30am to midnight. The rates are 15 Kr ($2.65) per bag or 20 Kr ($3.50) per backpack per day. Alternatively, lockers are available for 10 Kr ($1.75) per day.

Den Danske Bank, on the station's platform side, is open daily from 7am to 9pm (to 10pm in summer). Commission rates are competitive with other area banks Monday, Wednesday, and Friday from 9:30am to 4pm and on Thursday from 9:30am to 6pm; rates rise from 23 Kr ($4) to 40 Kr ($7) outside these "normal" banking hours.

From June through September, travelers can relax and shower free at the **Interrail Center,** a popular meeting point for backpackers. It's open daily from 6am to 11pm.

Other station facilities include a supermarket, open daily from 8am to midnight; a post office, open Monday through Friday from 8am to 10pm, on Saturday from 9am to 4pm, and on Sunday from 10am to 5pm; and an international telephone bureau called **TeleCom,** open Monday through Friday from 8am to 10pm, on Saturday from 9am to 4pm, and on Sunday from 10am to 5pm.

At the train station, you may also rent bicycles, get a shoe shine, buy flowers, buy a paperback, get a meal (from good pizza at **City Pizza** to a delectable Danish buffet at the **Bistro**), and rent a luggage cart for a refundable 10 Kr ($1.75).

The city's **subway (S-tog)** lines converge at Central Station. Go to platforms 9 through 12 to catch one of these trains.

BY BUS

Out-of-town and airport buses arrive at and depart from Central Station, which, as its name implies, is centrally located. It's also a couple of blocks from the city's budget hotels.

BY CAR

From Europe, you will enter Denmark either from Germany or by car ferry from Sweden at Malmö or Helsingborg.

TOURIST INFORMATION

The **Danish Tourist Board,** H. C. Andersens Boulevard 22 (tel. 33/11-13-25), has been talking about moving, but for now is near the northeast corner of Tivoli Park, across from Town Hall. Their most useful publication is the free guide *Copenhagen This Week,* which is also available in hotels and tourist spots around town. Visit this office primarily for hostel information and specialized information on Copenhagen and all of Denmark. Otherwise, you'll do better at the Use-It office, mentioned below. The tourist board is open June to mid-September, Monday through Friday from 9am to 6pm, on Saturday from 9am to 4pm, and on Sunday and holidays from 9am to 1pm; mid-September through April, Monday through Friday from 9am to 5pm, and on Saturday from 9am to noon (closed Sunday); and May, Monday through Friday from 9am to 5pm, on Saturday 9am to 1pm, and Sunday 9am to 1pm. The office is closed December 24 and 31. To enter, walk past the admission counters for Louis Tussaud's Wax Museum and the Hologram Museum. The credit-card telephone (purportedly the most economical way to call home) in the left-hand corner accepts VISA and American Express.

Use-It, on the second floor of Huset, Rådhusstræde 13 (tel. 33/15-65-18), is Copenhagen's "alternative" information office. Although the office may appear youth oriented, the information is geared toward budget travelers of all ages and is often superior to that of the Danish Tourist Board. A number of useful and free publications are distributed here, including *Playtime,* a newspaper with advice on low-cost restaurants, hotels, and sightseeing activities; and a city map. The energetic young staff can counsel travelers on getting a job, renting an apartment, and almost anything else. Other useful services include a ride board for travelers needing rides or companions to other points in Europe and a terrific room-finding service (see Chapter 4, "Rooms in Private Homes"). Unfortunately, lines here can be very long, especially in summer, so unless you want to chat, head straight for the publications and move on. There is a big table where you may relax and read the materials; there's also a basket with condoms in it. Another handy service is a free locker for a day, with a 50 Kr ($8.80) refundable deposit; you may leave belongings for a longer period for 10 Kr ($1.75) per day. Use-It is open June 15 to September 14, daily from 9am to 7pm, the rest of the year, Monday through Friday only from 10am to 4pm.

THE COPENHAGEN CARD

Anyone planning to spend any time at all in Copenhagen should take advantage of the **Copenhagen Card,** which entitles holders to free entry to Tivoli and museums, free public transportation, and good discounts on a variety of activities throughout the city. The card is good for 1, 2, or 3 days and costs 105, 170, or 215 Kr ($18.40, $29.80, or $37.70), respectively. Children under 12 years of age pay half price. Cards may be bought at the Danish Tourist Board (see "Tourist Information," above), the Room Service booth in Central Station, and at many hotels and S-tog stations.

CITY LAYOUT

The heartbeat of Copenhagen is **Strøget,** a mile-long (1.8km) pedestrian zone that links the city's two major squares, **Rådhuspladsen** (City Hall Square) and **Kongens Nytorv** (King's New Square). Strøget is Copenhagen's most popular shopping venue as it brims with entertainment, history, and local color. Although this strip seems a centuries-old essential part of city life, it was only rid of automobiles in 1962. Lined with cafés and boutiques, Strøget is actually a chain of five streets: Østergade, Amagertorv, Vimmelskaftet, Nygade, and Frederiksberggade.

Kongens Nytorv is the site of the Royal Theater and the Magasin du Nord department store, Scandinavia's largest and grandest, and the beginning of **Nyhavn,** which means New Harbor. Actually a canal, it was built in 1671 to link the harbor to the square. Once the city's raucous sailors' quarter, it has become a pedestrian area, more nice than naughty, with fine restaurants interspersed with the occasional tattoo parlor and honky-tonk bar.

Gothersgade, a street just coming into its own, is an extension of Nyhavn, bordering Kongens Nytorv. Filled with interesting restaurants and shops, it also passes Rosenborg Castle and the Botanical Garden.

Købmagergade, another pedestrian avenue, branches off from the middle of Strøget at Amagertov, and itself spawns several smaller pedestrian streets as it twists its way north to **Kultorvet** (the Coal Square), where vendors from North Zealand once sold charcoal from their carts.

A new pedestrian street, called **Strædet,** runs parallel to Strøget, and, like it, is made up of several streets dating from the Middle Ages with long names that are real tongue twisters like Læderstræde and

Kompagnistræde. The street is known for its antiques shops, antiquarian book shops, and galleries, and is filled with houses built just prior to 1800, after an enormous fire swept through the area in 1795.

Rådhuspladsen, the large Town Hall Square at Strøget's western terminus, buzzes with activity day and night. Beyond it, the wide **Vesterbrogade** takes up where Strøget leaves off, continuing west past Tivoli, Central Station, and into the Frederiksberg section of the city. Many of the suggested hotels in this guide are clustered just southwest of Central Station on streets perpendicular to Vesterbrogade.

NEIGHBORHOODS IN BRIEF

Downtown Though now youth-oriented, downtown Copenhagen actually dates back to the Middle Ages. Downtown is bisected by Strøget, the mile-long pedestrian street, with Tivoli and Town Hall at one end, and Kongens Nytorv (King's New Square) at the other. Amalienborg and Rosenborg palaces are found downtown, along with many museums, churches, parks, gardens, and a string of four rectangular lakes.

Latin Quarter Located a few blocks north of Strøget via Fiolstræde and Købmagergade, the Latin Quarter is home to the university and many small shops, secondhand bookstores, bohemian hangouts, and a lively square called Kultorvet.

Nørrebro Continuing north via Frederiksberg past the lakes to Nørrebrogade is the up-and-coming neighborhood Nørrebro, sprouting ethnic restaurants and bars with live music. In this neighborhood, you'll also find the Workers Museum as well as Assistens Cemetery, the resting place for Hans Christian Andersen, Søren Kierkegaard, and other famous departed Copenhageners.

Østerbro Due east of Nørrebro (as its name indicates), Østerbro is home to Fælled Park, where many outdoor concerts are held in summer.

Vesterbro West of downtown, following Vesterbrogade from Town Hall, the Vesterbro area is filled with ethnic restaurants and less expensive shops; it is also home to the Carlsberg Brewery.

Frederiksberg Adjacent to Vesterbro, the Frederiksberg area has two parks, Søndermarken and Frederiksberg Have, tree-lined streets, and a number of private homes that rent rooms to travelers (see Chapter 4).

Langelinie The official emblem of the city, the Little Mermaid sits wistfully on rocks in the mouth of Copenhagen harbor beside Langelinie, the waterfront. (*Langelinie* means the "Long Line.") Visiting cruise ships and naval vessels dock here, and the Citadel (Kastellet) and old city ramparts, throwbacks to olden times, are close by.

Slotsholmen The thumbnail island of Slotsholmen (which

COPENHAGEN
City Layout

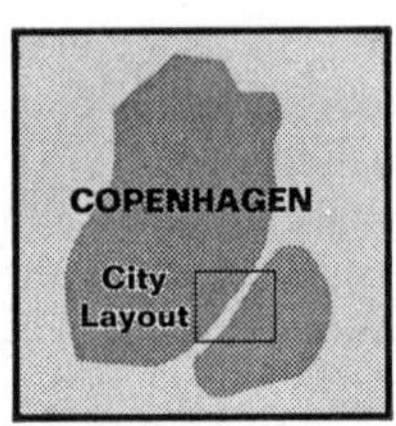

Amager 1
Christianshavn 2
Danish Tourist Board 15
Downtown 17
Gothersgade 5
Købmagergade 11
Kongens Nytorv 4
Kultorvet 6
Langelinie 9
Latin Quarter 12
Nørrebro 19
Nyhavn 3
Rådhuspladsen 13
Slotsholmen 20
Strøget 14
Vesterbro 18
Vesterbrogade 16

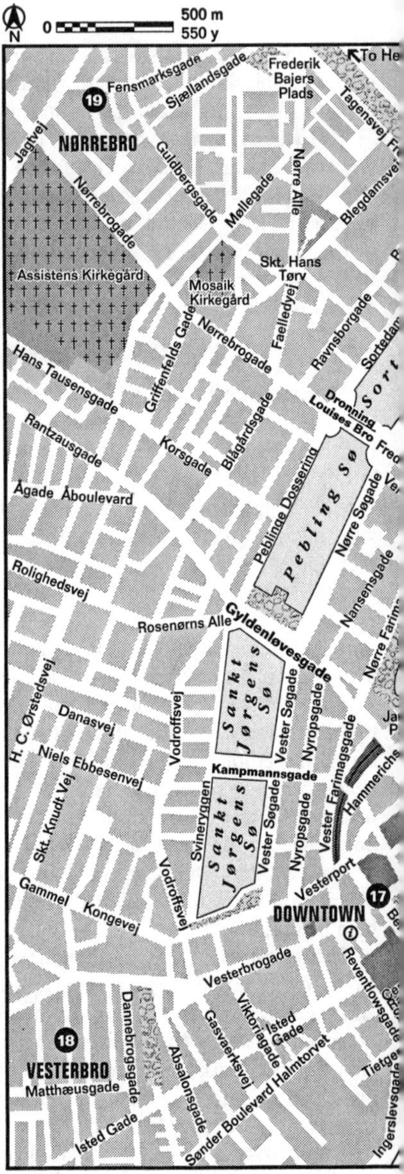

N
0
500 m
550 y
To He
Fensmarksgade
Sjællandsgade
Frederik Bajers Plads
Tagensvej
19
NØRREBRO
Jagtvej
Nørrebrogade
Guldbergsgade
Nørre Allé
Møllegade
Blegdamsvej
Skt. Hans Torv
Assistens Kirkegård
Mosaik Kirkegård
Griffenfelds Gade
Nørrebrogade
Faelledvej
Ravnsborgade
Hans Tausensgade
Dronning Louises Bro
Rantzausgade
Korsgade
Blågårdsgade
Peblinge Dossering
Peblinge Sø
Nørre Søgade
Ågade
Åboulevard
Rolighedsvej
Nansensgade
Rosenørns Alle
Gyldenløvesgade
Sankt Jørgens Sø
H. C. Ørstedsvej
Danasvej
Vodroffsvej
Vester Søgade
Nyropsgade
Niels Ebbesenvej
Kampmannsgade
Skt. Knudt Vej
Svineryggen
Vester Farimagsgade
Hammerichsgade
Gammel Kongevej
Vodroffsvej
Vesterport
17
DOWNTOWN
Vesterbrogade
Reventlowsgade
Dannebrogsgade
Gasvaerksvej
Viktoriagade
Isted Gade
18
VESTERBRO
Matthæusgade
Absalonsgade
Halmtorvet
Tietgen
Isted Gade
Sønder Boulevard
Ingerslevsgade

hardly seems an island, surrounded as it is by skinny canals and wedged tightly against the mainland) lies a few blocks south of Strøget at Højbro Plads and contains Christiansborg Palace, the National Library, and a number of museums.

Christianshavn Just south of Slotsholmen, across Knippels

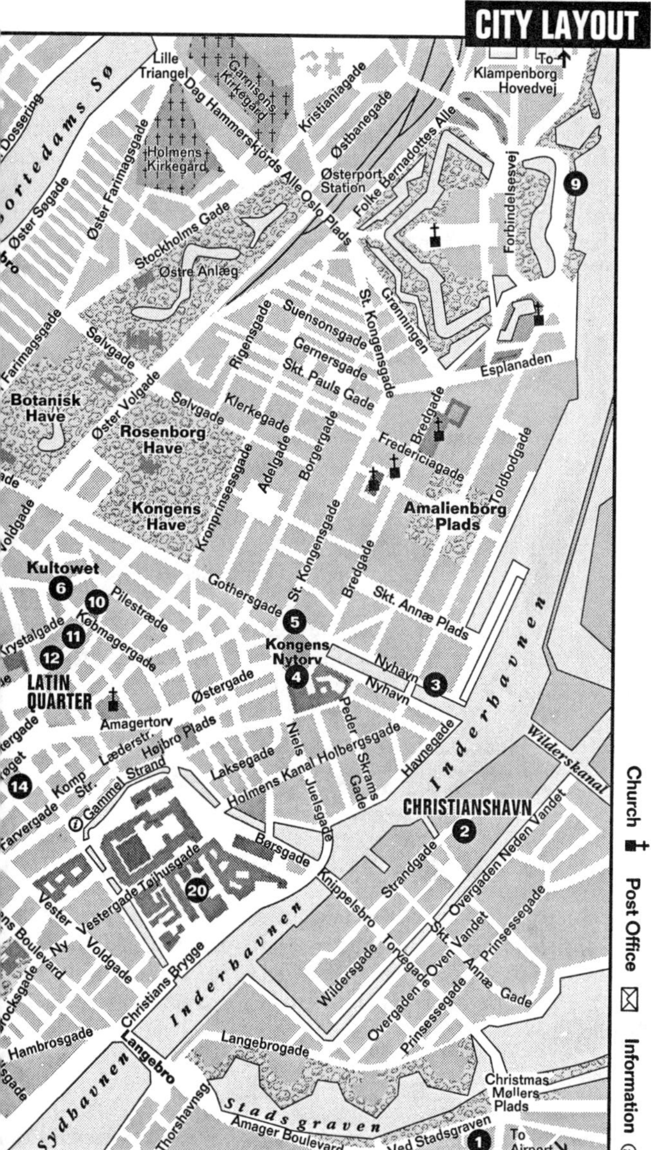

Bridge, is Christianshavn (Christian's Harbor), founded by King Christian IV early in the 1700s as a community for merchants and as a buffer zone for the city against sea attacks. Laid out Dutch-style with picturesque canals, Christianshavn has three unique points of interest: the Church of Our Saviour, Christian's Church, and Christiania, the counterculture community that sprang up here in 1971 and has been entrenched ever since (see "Walking Tour 4" in Chapter 7).

Amager Just beyond Christianshavn lies the much larger island of Amager, not really a tourist draw, except for: a narrow strip of park at the water's edge opposite Christianshavn; Copenhagen Airport on its eastern shore, six miles southeast of Copenhagen; and Dragør, a fishing village south of the airport, with narrow streets and tiny houses. Dutch farmers once inhabited most of Amager, making their livelihood by selling vegetables to the city dwellers of Copenhagen.

STREET MAPS

Maps are easy to come by in Copenhagen, and they are free and easy to decipher. Two serviceable ones are printed in back of *Copenhagen This Week:* one of the downtown area, with the major attractions and pedestrian streets well marked; and the other of Greater Copenhagen, indicating bus routes and S-tog stops. The Copenhagen Tourist Association publishes a big Map of Wonderful Copenhagen, and Use-It distributes a still bigger and possibly better map (see "Tourist Information," above).

Many streets in Copenhagen are blessedly short (even mile-long Strøget is made up of five short streets), so you won't spend precious time traipsing around looking for an address.

2. GETTING AROUND

BY PUBLIC TRANSPORTATION

It's a given: Trains and buses run regularly, and bus drivers get a gold star for helpfulness; local transportation is free for holders of the Copenhagen Card (see "The Copenhagen Card," above). As of 1991, the city even loans out bikes for free to help you get around (see "By Bicycle," below).

SAVING MONEY

If you plan on traveling by train or bus a lot, buy an 11-ticket strip for 80 Kr ($14.05). Tickets can be bought on buses and at all rail stations. Children under 12 always ride for half price; those under 7 ride free.

Dial 31/95-17-01 for bus information and 33/14-17-01 for S-tog information, 24 hours.

If you buy the **Copenhagen Card,** your local travel expenses are covered (see "The Copenhagen Card," above).

BY SUBWAY (S-TOG)

Copenhagen is served by an extensive bus and subway network. Regular service begins daily at 5am (at 6am on Sunday) and continues until 12:20am. At other times there is a limited night-bus service departing from Town Hall Square.

Fares are based on a zone system; the farther you go the more you pay. Most destinations in central Copenhagen will cost the minimum 8 Kr ($1.40). Buses and subway trains use the same tickets and you can transfer as much as you like for up to 1 hour.

The subway—called the S-tog—works on the honor system. Either pay your fare in the station you're departing from, or stamp your own strip ticket in the yellow box on the platform. In Central Station, the S-tog departs from platforms 9 through 12.

BY BUS

Buses are frequent, and bus routes are extensive and well marked on Map 3 in back of *Copenhagen This Week*. When you board a bus, either pay the driver, stamp your ticket in the machine, or flash your Copenhagen Card. It's easy to get away without paying, but beware: Fines for fare dodging are stiff.

Bus drivers are exceptionally nice. Most speak some English, and even if they don't, they have an uncanny ability to decipher your destination and help you get there.

BY TAXI

Unless you've got money to burn, don't even think about taking a cab—except for short distances. Remember that the tip is factored into the fare.

The basic taxi fare is 12 Kr ($2.10) at the flag drop (make sure your cab has a meter), then 7.20 Kr ($1.26) per kilometer (.62 mile) between 6am and 6pm, or 9.6 Kr ($1.68) between 6pm and 6am and on Saturday and Sunday. Payment by credit card is acceptable. A cab available for hire displays the word *FRI*. To order a taxi in advance, dial 31/10-10-10 or 31/35-35-35.

BY CAR

Unless you're planning an extended trip outside Copenhagen, you will find that keeping a car in the city is more trouble than it's worth, especially after you tally the cost of a car rental, gas, and parking (see following sections).

As Copenhagen's public transportation is reasonably priced, readily available, quick, and efficient, there is little need to rent a car for city use only.

IMPRESSIONS

I see here nothing but heaps of ruins, and only converse with people immersed in trade and sensuality.
—MARY WOLLSTONECRAFT, 1795

RENTALS

Car-rental companies enforce a minimum-age requirement, which ranges from 20 to 25, depending on the company; the driver must also have a valid driver's license, along with an international driver's license. Figure on spending about $100 a day, including insurance, 22% VAT, and unlimited mileage; or $200 a week plus 22% VAT, and $15 insurance a day. Special weekend rates run about $120. When booking an air or rail ticket, it's possible to book a rental car as well.

To get the best bargain, compare the rates of the big-name rental companies versus the smaller local companies. Possibilities include **Avis,** 1 Kampmannsgade (tel. 33/15-22-99); **Budget,** 6 Nyropsgade (tel. 33/13-39-00); **Hertz,** 3 Ved Vesterport (tel. 33/12-77-00); **interRent/EuropCar,** 6 Jernbanegade (tel. 33/11-62-00); and **Pitzner,** 4 Trommesalen (tel. 33/11-12-34). All of the above have branches at Copenhagen Airport.

For the most up-to-date car-rental information, check the "Transport" section of *Copenhagen This Week.*

If you belong to the **American Automobile Association (AAA),** take advantage of a Danish auto association that has a reciprocal agreement with AAA (there are several).

PARKING

Parking forbudt means "no parking," but it may apply only to certain times of the day, so check the sign. *Datoparkering* means that "parking is allowed only on one side of the street"—on the side with even numbers on even dates, and odd numbers on odd dates. In downtown Copenhagen, there is one-hour-only curbside parking weekdays from 9am to 5pm, and Saturday until 1pm unless otherwise indicated.

Parking meters downtown cost 15 Kr ($2.65) per hour, with a three-hour limit. The fee is 40% to 70% less as you get farther away from the city center. For parking lots and garages in Copenhagen, check listings in *Copenhagen This Week.*

DRIVING RULES

All car passengers—including those in the back seat—must buckle their seat belts, and drivers must use their lights even in daytime.

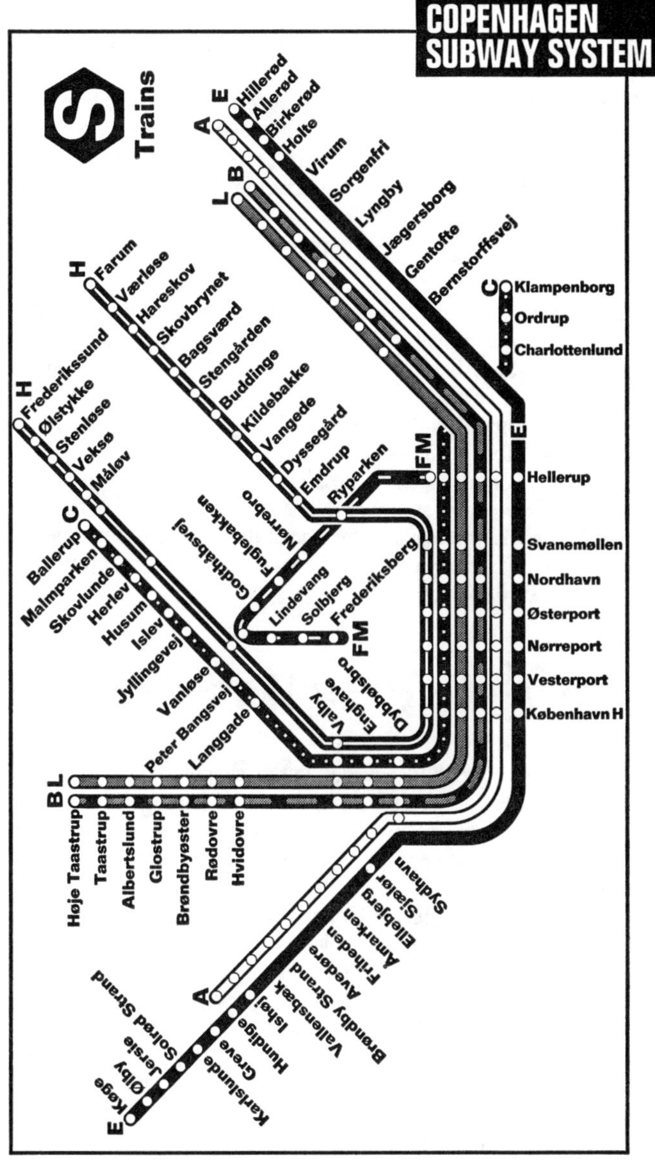

Remember that Copenhagen is filled with bicyclists and pedestrians, so always keep an eye out for them, especially at crossings.

If you need car service, day or night, call **Falck,** (tel. 33/14-22-22); there is a charge for towing, if it's necessary.

ON FOOT

The compact city center and many pedestrian thoroughfares make walking a breeze. You may be interested in picking up a copy of "Copenhagen on Foot," a well-written booklet of walking tours distributed free by Use-It (see "Tourist Information," above).

BY BICYCLE

Wide bike lanes, long green traffic lights, and beautiful surroundings encourage bike riding for both recreational and transportation purposes. About half of all Danes ride regularly, and even high government officials can sometimes be seen pedaling to work. A guide to biking in and around Copenhagen is distributed free by Use-It (see "Tourist Information," above).

Proof of Copenhageners' hospitality and respect for bicyclists is the city's free bike-loan program begun in May 1991. With a 20Kr ($3.50) deposit, you may borrow one of the 5,000 bicycles; when you return the bike to any one of 800 racks around the city, you receive your deposit back.

COPENHAGEN

Airport See "Orientation" in this chapter.

American Express The American Express office is conveniently located in the middle of Strøget, at Amagertorv 18 (tel. 33/11-50-05). It is open weekdays from 9am to 5pm and on Saturday from 9am to noon.

Area Codes When dialing local numbers in Copenhagen, always include the area code, which for numbers most often called by tourists is 31 or 33; thus, local numbers have eight digits. The city code for Copenhagen is 45 when calling from outside Denmark.

Baby-sitters Minerva [Students] is a multilingual baby-sitter clearinghouse charging 25 Kr ($4.40) per hour, plus a 25-Kr ($4.40) booking fee. Reserve Monday through Thursday from 6 to 9am and 3 to 6pm, on Friday from 3 to 7pm only (tel. 31/22-96-96). On Saturday the office is open from 3 to 5pm only. The student sitters are of all ages.

Banks Banks are usually open Monday through Friday from 10am to 4pm (on Thursday until 6pm). Outside these hours, the best place to change money is either the American Express office, Amagertorv 18 at Hemmingsens Gade (tel. 33/11-50-05), open

Monday through Friday from 9am to 5pm, and on Saturday from 9am to noon; or the exchange office in Central Station, open daily from 7am to 9pm (until 10pm from April through September).

Bookstores Copenhagen has a wealth of bookstores, called *boghandel,* that carry a good selection of travel books, as well as fiction and nonfiction books in English. Tops among them are **Boghallen,** in the Politiken building, Rådhuspladsen 37, a block from Strøget (tel. 33/11-85-11), and **Arnold Busck,** Købmagergade 49 (tel. 33/12-24-53). Prices for paperbacks range from 49 to 99 Kr ($8.60 to $17.35).

Business Hours **Shops** are usually open Monday through Thursday from 9am to 5:30pm (department stores until 6pm), on Friday from 9am until 7 or 8pm, and on Saturday from 9am until 1 or 2pm (the first Saturday of the month until 5pm). **Offices** are open Monday through Friday from 9 or 10am until 4 or 5pm, and sometimes on Saturday until noon or 1pm.

Car Rentals See "Getting Around" in this chapter.

Climate See "When to Go" in Chapter 2.

Currency See "Information, Entry Requirements & Money" in Chapter 2.

Currency Exchange The best place to change money is a bank. It's also possible to do it at the airport. **Boghallen,** the bookstore in the Politiken building, Rådhuspladsen 37, accepts traveler's checks and gives a good rate of exchange on them.

Dentists Emergency dental care is provided by **Tandlægevagten,** Oslo Plads 14 (tel. 31/38-02-51). The office, located near Østerport Station, is open weekdays from 8am to 9:30pm, and 10am to noon on Saturday, Sunday, and holidays.

Doctors To reach a doctor outside normal hours, dial 33/93-63-00 weekdays from 8am to 4pm; otherwise, call 33/12-00-41.

Documents Required See "Information, Entry Requirements & Money" in Chapter 2.

Driving Rules See "Getting Around" in this chapter.

Drugstores Twenty-four-hour services are provided by centrally located **Steno Apotek,** Vesterbrogade 6C (tel. 33/14-82-66), and near the center but on Amager, **Sønderbro Apotek,** Amagerbrogade 158 (tel. 31/58-01-40).

Electricity 220 volts, so you'll need a converter, as well as an adapter with two thin round prongs (opposed to the flat prongs, as in the United States and Canada).

Embassies Denmark's capital is home to the embassies of many nations, including: the **U.S. Embassy,** Dag Hammerskjölds Allé 24 (tel. 31/42-31-44); the **Canadian Embassy,** Kristen Bernikowsgade 1 (tel. 33/12-22-99); the **British Embassy,** Kastelsvej 40 (tel. 31/26-46-00); **Irish Embassy,** Østbanegade

21 (tel. 31/42-32-33); and the **Australian Embassy,** Kristianiagade 21 (tel. 31/26-22-44). The nearest embassy of New Zealand is in The Hague, Netherlands.

Emergencies Dial 000 for **police, fire, or ambulance** service. No coins are needed when dialing from a public phone. **Steno Apotek,** Vesterbrogade 6C (tel. 33/14-82-66), is a 24-hour pharmacy located just across from Central Station.

Etiquette Keep in mind that the Danes tend to be more subdued in public than Americans. You may want to try eating the way the Danes do: with a knife and fork in unison, not with the fork only. This includes smørrebrod and pizza. Watch the Danes, you'll get the hang of it. Water is not served automatically in restaurants, so you have to request it, and waiters are happy to bring it. If you are fortunate enough to be invited to a dinner party in a Danish home, always wait for the host to *skal* before taking a drink. You *skal* with wine, never with beer.

Eyeglasses Several optical shops are located in and around Strøget. **Synoptik,** Købmagergade 22 (tel. 33/15-05-38), has a particularly large selection of modern frames. It's open Monday through Thursday from 9:30am to 6pm, on Friday from 9:30am to 7pm, and on Saturday from 9:30am to 2pm.

Haircuts Go to **Harpelund,** Gammel Kongevej 142, in Frederiksberg (tel. 31/31-23-01). Women pay about 200 Kr ($35) for a cut; men, 185 Kr ($32.45). No tip is expected.

Holidays See "When to Go" in Chapter 2.

Hospitals Even foreigners staying temporarily in Denmark are entitled to free hospital care in the event of a sudden illness. **Rigshospitalet,** Blegdamsvej 9, is the most centrally located hospital (tel. 31/38-66-33).

Information See "Information, Entry Requirements & Money" in Chapter 2; see also "Orientation," above, in this chapter.

Language Pick up Berlitz's pocket-size *Danish for Travellers,* available in the travel section of most bookstores. It gives you the pronunciation of handy phrases for situations travelers typically find themselves in, and it is color coded according to subject. (See also Appendix A.)

Laundry/Dry Cleaning Copenhagen has dozens of laundries in all different areas of town; look for the word *vask* (wash) such as *møntvask* or *vaskeri.* **Vask-Mønt-Vask,** Holbergsgade 9, just a few blocks from the Royal Palace, is open daily from 6am to 10pm. It costs about 30 Kr ($5.25) to do a load of wash.

For dry cleaning, go to Vester Farimagsgade 3 (tel. 33/12-45-45), just one block from Central Station. It's open Monday through Friday from 8am to 6pm, but it's not cheap at about 150 Kr ($26.30) for a suit, shirt, and tie.

Library **Hoved Biblioteket,** Kultorvet 2, is the main public library. It's open Monday through Thursday from 11am to 7pm, on Friday from 11am until 5pm, and on Saturday from 10am to 2pm (tel. 33/93-60-60).

Liquor Laws The legal drinking age in Denmark is 18. Alcohol is sold all over, including in grocery stores and at gas stations.

Lost Property If you lost it on a train or bus, try the **Lost Property Office** at Lyshojgardsvej 80, Valby (tel. 36/44-20-10 for trains, 31/46-01-44 for buses). It's open Monday through Friday from 10am to 5pm. If you lost it somewhere else, try the **Copenhagen police** at Carl Jacobsensvej 20, Valby (tel. 31/16-14-06), open Monday through Friday from 9am to 3pm (on Thursday until 5pm).

Luggage Storage/Lockers Luggage storage is available at Copenhagen Airport and the central railway station in downtown Copenhagen. The latter also has plenty of lockers. For charges, see "Orientation" and "Getting Around" in this chapter.

Mail The main post office is at Tietgensgade 37, and there's another post office at Købmagergade 33—both of these are open Monday through Friday, 9am to 6pm, Saturday 9am to 1pm. Letters weighing under 20 grams cost 4.75 Kr (83¢) to North America and Australia; postcards require 3.75 Kr (66¢). It takes two weeks for mail to reach the United States.

You can receive mail marked "Poste Restante" most conveniently (in terms of location and hours) at the post office in the central train station, Monday through Friday from 8am to 10pm, Saturday 9am to 4pm, and Sunday 10am to 5pm. Holders of American Express cards or traveler's checks can pick up personal mail at that company's main office (see "Banks" above). American Express will hold mail for 30 days and forward it for 35 Kr ($6.14), but the company does not accept parcels.

Maps See "Street Maps" above.

Money See "Information, Entry Requirements & Money" in Chapter 2.

Newspapers/Magazines There are no English-language newspapers printed in Denmark. However, the *International Herald Tribune, USA Today,* and other papers are widely available. Newsstands on Nytorv (Strøget), across from Town Hall, and in major hotels have good selections.

You can read newspapers and magazines free at **Hoved Biblioteket,** the main public library (see "Library," above).

Photographic Needs Film and batteries are available at **Kontant Foto,** Købmagergade 43 (tel. 33/93-60-60), the largest camera supply and photo store in Copenhagen. It's open Monday through Friday from 10am to 7pm, and on Saturday from 10am to 2pm. **Foto Quick,** in Rådhusarkaden, at H. C. Andersens Boulevard and Vesterbrogade, offers one-hour processing but exacts a hefty price: 118 Kr ($20.70) for 24 exposures, 165 Kr ($28.95) for 36 exposures; it's open Monday through Friday from 9am to 5:30pm, Saturday until 2pm. A roll of film (36 exposures, 100 ASA) generally costs about 63 Kr ($11.05).

Police In an emergency, dial 000 from any phone. No coins are needed. For other police matters, call Police Headquarters, Polititorvet (tel. 33/14-14-48).

Post Office See "Mail" above.

Radio English-language newscasts are broadcast Monday through Friday at 8:10am on 90.8 FM.

Religious Services The **Cathedral of Copenhagen** (Danish Protestant), Nørregade, is Denmark's most important church; Sunday services are held at 10am and 5pm and Friday at 11am. The **Christian Church Copenhagen,** Gammel Kongevej 13 (tel. 31/75-07-01), is an interdenominational Protestant church with services in English. **Catholic services** are held at **St. Ansgar Church,** Bredgade 64 (tel. 33/13-37-62), Saturday at 5pm and Sunday at 10am; Catholic services in English are held at **Sankt Annæ Kirke,** Hans Bogbinders Allé 2 (tel. 31/58-21-02), on Saturday and Sunday at 5pm; take bus 2 or 13. The largest **Jewish synagogue** is at Krystalgade 12 (tel. 33/12-88-68). The **Muslim Cultural Institute,** Vesterbrogade 107 (tel. 31/24-67-86), holds services and acts as a resource center for Copenhagen's Islamic community. The city's "gay church," **Metropolitan Community Church,** Knabrostræde 3 (tel. 31/83-32-86), has services in Danish on Sunday at 5pm; the minister, Mia Andersen, speaks English.

Rest Rooms Danes call them "toilets" in English, *toilettet* in Danish, and they are available in department stores, such as Illums on Strøget, and in the Scala entertainment/shopping/dining complex on Vesterbrogade. (*Hvor er toilettet?* is Danish for "Where is the toilet?")

Safety As large cities go, Copenhagen is a haven of safety. Take the usual precautions you would take in any unfamiliar city or country: Stay alert and be conscious of your immediate surroundings; wear a moneybelt and keep a special eye on cameras, purses, and wallets—items that say "come hither" to pickpockets and other scofflaws; and be particularly careful on dimly lit streets and in parks at dusk or after dark.

Shoe Repair **Hælebaren,** Frederiksberggade 4 (tel. 33/12-74-31), is a well-located shoe-repair shop near the beginning of Strøget; it's open Monday through Thursday from 8am to 5:30pm, on Friday from 8am to 7pm, and on Saturday from 9am to 2pm. There is also a shoe-repair shop in Cityarkaden, near the end of Strøget, at Østergade 32 (tel. 31/91-02-20); as well as **Mister Minit** (tel. 33/11-21-08) in the center of Central Station, which is open from 8am to 8pm weekdays and 9am to 6pm weekends.

Sundries The **grocery store** in Cityarkaden, Østergade 32, can supply miscellaneous items such as towels, socks, underwear, wine, candles, and portable snacks. **DæIls Varehus** department store, Nørregade 12 (tel. 31/12-78-25), has anything else you might need. Postcards, which are expensive in Copenhagen, cost only 1 Kr each at **København Souvenir,** Frederiksberggade 28 (Strøget).

Tax Denmark's 22% Value Added Tax is called MOMS (pronounced "mumps"), and is usually included in the prices listed in hotel tariffs and restaurant menus. Many stores offer tourists the opportunity to reclaim sales tax on purchases over 600 Kr ($105.30). See Chapter 8 for details.

Taxis Recommended for short trips only. See "Getting Around," above.

Telephone/Telex/Fax In Copenhagen always remember to dial the area code first—even for local calls. The first two digits are the area code, and they are followed by another six digits, which are the local number. (See also "Area Codes," above, and "Useful Telephone Numbers," below.)

Local telephone calls cost a minimum of 50 øre (9¢) for about 2½ minutes. Deposit either two 25-øre coins, or splurge on a whole krone; a tone will sound when you have to add more coins. On older phones, deposit coins before dialing; although unused coins are not returned even if you reach a busy signal, they are credited toward another call. On newer phones—recognizable by their yellow front plate—wait for the answering party to pick up before inserting money. Local **directory assistance** is 0033.

It costs five times as much to make a local call from a hotel room as it does from a pay phone, which you will usually find in the hotel lobby.

As for **international calls,** it costs 13 Kr ($2.30) per minute to call the United States. The easiest way to call North America is via AT&T's "USA Direct" service. If you have an AT&T Calling Card, or call collect, you can reach an American operator from any phone by dialing 08001-0010. Deposit 50 øre before dialing. Alternatively, you can make long-distance calls from the Central Station's TeleCom Center (tel. 33/14-20-00), located inside the station; it's open Monday through Friday from 8am to 10pm, on Saturday from 9am to 4pm, and on Sunday from 10am to 5pm.

Television Resign yourself to understanding little; most programming is in Danish and Swedish.

Time There is a six-hour time difference between Denmark and the east coast of the United States (Eastern standard time). Daylight saving time is in effect in Denmark from the end of March until the end of September.

Tipping A 15% service charge is automatically added to most restaurant bills. If service has been extraordinary, you might want to round up the bill. Tipping is the exception—not the rule—in Denmark.

Transit Information For S-tog trains, call 33/14-17-01; for buses, 31/95-17-01. Bus drivers are extremely helpful in getting you to your destination—most speak English.

Useful Telephone Numbers **Alcoholics Anonymous** (tel. 33/81-81-92) has meetings in English, Sunday at 10:30am and 2pm, and Wednesday at 7:30pm, at Ryesgade 107, which runs parallel to the artificial Sortedams Lake. **AIDS information** tel. 33/91-11-19; **police, fire,** or **ambulance** dial 000. (See also "Area Codes" and "Telephone/Telex/Fax," above).

Water The water is quite safe to drink in Copenhagen and throughout Denmark. You must request water in restaurants—it is not automatically served.

3. NETWORKS & RESOURCES

FOR STUDENTS

Huset, Rådhusstræde 13 (tel. 33/32-00-66), is a unique city-subsidized building completely dedicated to students and young people. The building houses an information office, cafés, restaurants, and evening music spots, several of which are listed elsewhere in this book under their appropriate headings. The Use-It office (see "Tourist Information," above) also makes its home here, and shouldn't be missed.

Danish language courses are readily available from several sources in Copenhagen, among them **K.I.S.S. (the Danish Language School),** Nørregade 20 (tel. 31/11-44-77), where courses last 2½ weeks and cost 168 Kr ($29.50), including materials. Ask for the "Danish Courses for Foreigners" pamphlet at the Use-It office.

Den Internationale Højskole (an international folk high school), Montebello Allé 1, DK-3000 Helsingør (tel. 32/21-33-61), has a multilingual staff and offers courses in English and other languages (see "Alternative/Adventure Travel" in Chapter 2).

Transalpino, Skoubogade 6 (tel. 33/14-46-33), specializes in discount train and plane tickets for travelers under 26. **DIS,** Skindergade 28 (tel. 33/11-00-44), also offers bus, train, plane, and boat discounts to students and people under 26. There is a travel library/bookstore next door called Kopeen, where you can research

IMPRESSIONS

If you want to fling yourself on the mercy of anyone, pick a Dane.
—ARTICLE IN *TRAVEL & LEISURE*, 1988

your upcoming journeys and check a ride board for travel companions. Both offices are open Monday through Friday from 10am to 5pm.

The main building of **Copenhagen University,** dating from 1479, is right in the heart of the city next to Copenhagen Cathedral. Like many urban schools, the campus lacks the bustle and energy of student life; students prefer to hang out in nearby cafés.

FOR GAY MEN & LESBIANS

The best source of information about gay and lesbian activities in Copenhagen is the **Pan Center,** and more specifically its bookstore, called the **Bøgcafe,** Knabrostræde 3 (tel. 33/32-49-08). The staff is knowledgeable about gay goings-on and meeting places in the city and will give you the free "Copenhagen Gay Guide" and the monthly gay newspaper *Pan-Bladet*. Besides books, many in English, the shop also sells magazines, postcards, and posters, and there's usually coffee available for a small charge.

Just across the portal from the Bøgcafe, the Gay Center **library** (tel. 33/11-19-61) has books and periodicals from all over the world; it's open Monday through Friday from 5 to 7pm (until 8pm on Wednesday), and Saturday from 1pm to 3pm.

There is also a **general information number** that may be called weeknights only from 8pm to midnight: 33/13-01-12. The **AIDS information** number is 33/91-11-19.

The city's "gay church" is the **Metropolitan Community Church,** Knabrostræde 3 (tel. 31/83-32-86). Services, on Sunday at 5pm, are in Danish; but the minister, Mia Andersen, speaks excellent English.

FOR WOMEN

Kvindehuset (Women's House), Gothersgade 37 (tel. 33/14-28-04), is not—as the name may lead you to believe—a refuge for battered women. Rather, it is a center for women's exchange, informal discussions, and scheduled seminars and classes. There's a small but selective thrift shop on the premises, as well as tables and chairs where you may sit and share coffee and conversation with other women. The Women's House is open Monday through Friday from noon to 6pm; its café is open Monday and Thursday from 6pm to 10pm.

CHAPTER 4

COPENHAGEN ACCOMMODATIONS

The budget traveler will be happy to learn that Copenhagen offers several alternatives in accommodations, the most economical of which is renting a room in a private home. The hotels clustered around the railroad station tend to be the best bets—budgetwise. Room rates include a tax, which is 22% (at time of press). Breakfast is only included in the room rate when noted; when it is you're in for a treat, as a Danish breakfast buffet is a delicious and satisfying start to any day of sightseeing. It's advisable to reserve a room (in the case of a hostel, a bed) in advance if your stay in Copenhagen will be during the summer months, as this is when Copenhagen is inundated with visitors.

Room Service (Værelseanvisning), located near the east end of Central Station (tel. 33/12-28-80), specializes in booking private rooms, as well as same-day discounted hotel rooms. The office rents up to 160 private rooms, most of which are 10 to 15 minutes by bus or S-tog from the city center, with rates rarely topping 150 Kr ($26.30) per person. Room Service also works with some of the best hotels in the city, selling same-day space that would otherwise remain empty. There is a 13-Kr ($2.30) per-person booking fee and a small deposit required at time of booking. Hotels (not private homes) may be booked in advance by writing to Hotelbooking København, Hovedbanegården, DK-1570 København V. It's open May through August, daily from 9am to midnight; in September, daily from 9am to 10pm; in April and October, Monday through Saturday from 9am to 5pm; and November through March, Monday through Friday from 9am to 5pm and on Saturday from 9am to noon.

1. DOUBLES FOR LESS THAN 300 KR ($52.65)

IN THE CENTER

HOTEL KFUM SOLDATERHJEM, Gothersgade 115, København K. Tel. 33/15-40-44. 10 rms (none with bath). **S-tog:** Nørreport.

$ Rates: 175 Kr ($30.70) single; 290 Kr ($50.90) double. Cash only.

Although it was originally intended for soldiers, KFUM Soldaterhjem has been taken over by businesspeople and budget travelers searching for the best value in town. Rooms (8 singles, 2 doubles) here are devoid of decoration, but are spick-and-span clean. The reception, on the second floor, doubles as a piano lounge and snack bar (serving short-order meals for less than $5). Rooms are on the fifth floor, a hearty climb.

Rosenborg Castle is across the street from the hotel, and the clean-cut young men of the Royal Guard hang out in the lounge. Reception hours are 8:30am to 11pm Monday through Saturday, and 3 to 11pm Sundays and holidays; enter the door marked "Soldaterhjem." The hotel and café are run by the friendly, competent husband-and-wife team, Preben Nielsen and Grethe Thomasen.

NEAR THE CENTER

HOTEL 9 SMÅ HJEM, Classensgade 40, DK-2100 København Ø. Tel. 31/26-16-47. 60 rms (a few with shower, sink, and toilet). TV **Bus:** No. 40 from Central Station to Classensgade.

$ Rates (including breakfast, except where noted): 155 Kr ($27.20) single, without breakfast, summer only; the rest of the year 273 Kr ($47.90) single with bath, 180 Kr ($31.60) without bath; 110 Kr ($19.30) per person for two to five people, without breakfast, summer only; the rest of the year 385 Kr ($67.55) double with bath, 286 Kr ($50.20) without bath. Weekly rates year round: 1,484 Kr ($260.35) single with bath, 1,008 Kr ($176.85) single without bath; 2,058 Kr ($361.05) double with bath, 1,715 Kr ($300.90) double without bath. Apartments with kitchen or breakfast included are also available. ACCESS, DC, EURO, MC, V.

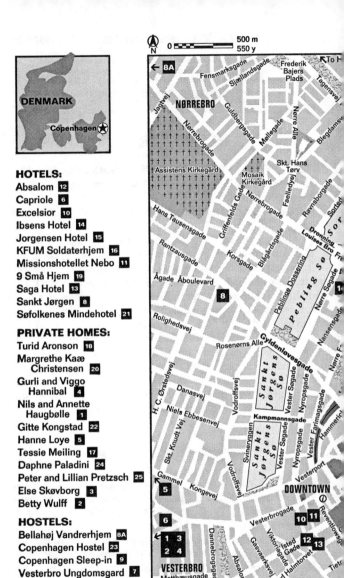

HOTELS:

- Absalom 12
- Capriole 6
- Excelsior 10
- Ibsens Hotel 14
- Jorgensen Hotel 15
- KFUM Soldaterhjem 16
- Missionshotellet Nebo 11
- 9 Små Hjem 19
- Saga Hotel 13
- Sankt Jørgen 8
- Søfolkenes Mindehotel 21

PRIVATE HOMES:

- Turid Aronson 18
- Margrethe Kaæ Christensen 20
- Gurli and Viggo Hannibal 4
- Nils and Annette Haugbølle 1
- Gitte Kongstad 22
- Hanne Loye 5
- Tessie Meiling 17
- Daphne Paladini 24
- Peter and Lillian Pretzsch 25
- Else Skøvborg 3
- Betty Wulff 2

HOSTELS:

- Bellahøj Vandrerhjem 8A
- Copenhagen Hostel 23
- Copenhagen Sleep-in 9
- Vesterbro Ungdomsgard 7

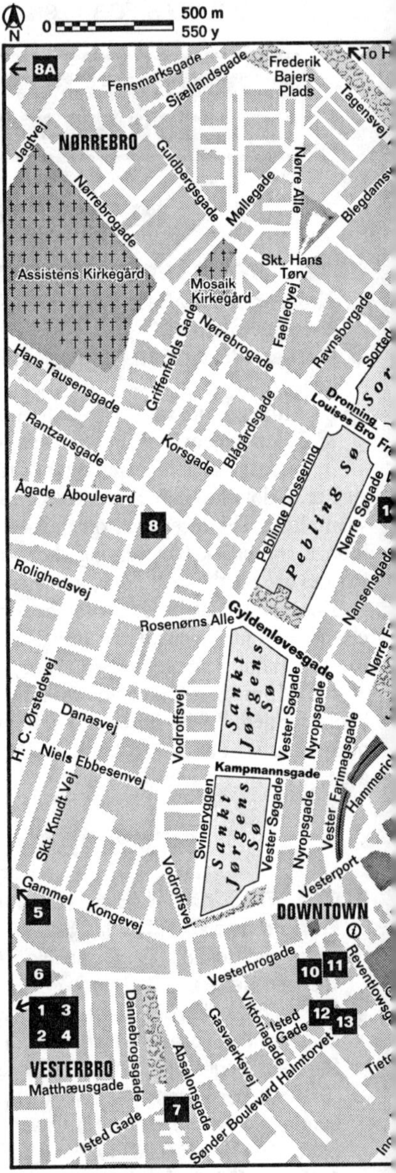

Clean, attractive, spacious rooms make this hotel (named "9 Small Homes") the best value in town, especially since most rates include breakfast, summer rates are low, and there's a kitchen on each floor for guests' use. Contemporary furniture, stately wall maps and prints, and modern conveniences like

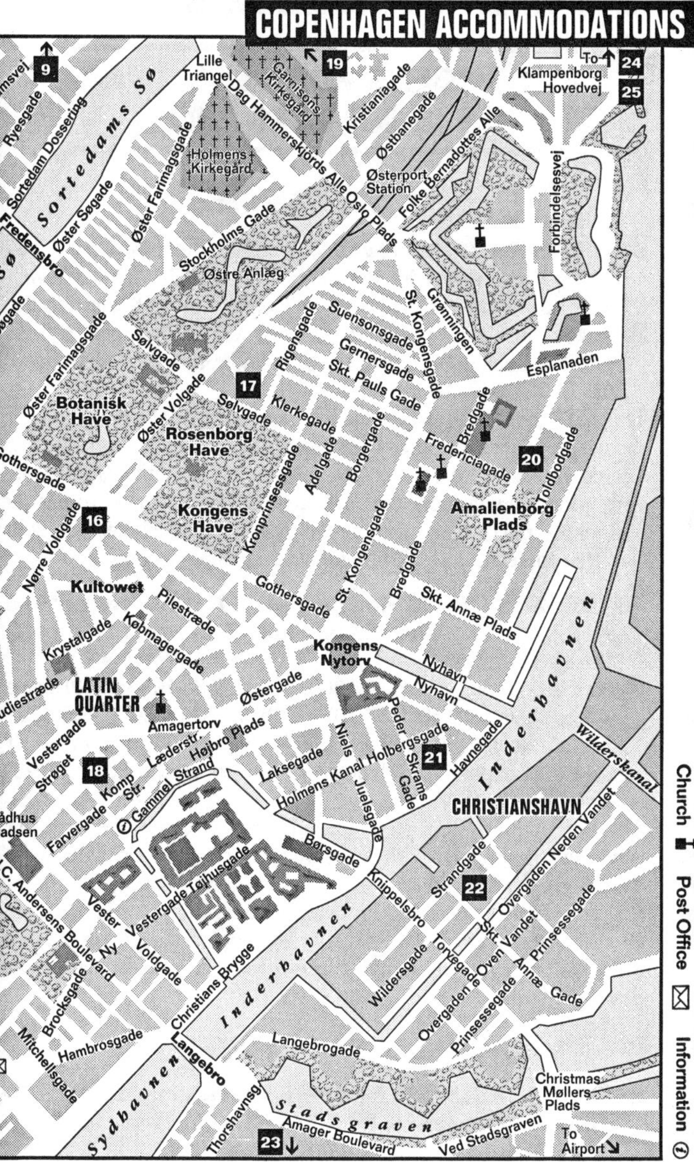

TVs and direct-dial phones make this an unbelievable find. What's the catch? The reception hours are limited to weekdays from 8am to 5:30pm, and maid service is available at an additional cost. There is no sign marking the building and the reception is on the third floor.

2. DOUBLES FOR LESS THAN 435 KR ($76.30)

IN THE CENTER

SØFOLKENES MINDEHOTEL, Peder Skrams Gade 19, 1054 København K. Tel. 33/13-48-82. 70 rms (none with bath). **Bus:** No. 4, 27, or 28 from Central Station to Havnegade.

$ Rates (including breakfast): 225 Kr ($39.50) single; 390 Kr ($68.40) double; 559 Kr ($98.10) triple; 660 Kr ($115.80) quad. AE, EURO, MC, V.

This hotel for Danish sailors and international travelers boasts one of the best locations in the city, just two blocks from Nyhavn and the Opera, and close to Strøget. Rooms are modest but comfortable, with good reading light; each has a sink. The 42 single rooms (at reasonable rates) make this a particularly good choice for solo travelers; there are also 17 doubles and 11 family rooms.

JORGENSEN HOTEL, Rømersgade 11, 1362 København K. Tel. 33/13-81-86. Fax 33/15-51-05. 22 rms (15 with bath). **S-tog:** Nørreport.

$ Rates (including breakfast): 200–310 Kr ($35.10–$54.40) single without bath, 500 Kr ($87.70) with bath; 300–450 Kr ($52.65–$78.95) double without bath, 600 Kr ($105.25) with bath; 80 Kr ($14.05) per person, cash only, in dorm rooms, plus 30 Kr ($5.25) extra for sheets. V.

This hotel, a block from pretty Ørsteds Park, welcomes everyone, but is particularly popular with gay travelers and youth hostel devotees. The rooms are basic, with a sink and little decoration. Dorm rooms have four to eight beds and lockers. The bathrooms could use more attention from the cleaning staff. The hotel's Café Adagio often hosts a drag show. Enter the hotel at the corner. A Laundromat is just down the street.

NEAR THE CENTER

HOTEL SANKT JØRGEN, Julius Thomsensgade 22, DK-1632 København V. Tel. 31/37-15-11. 20 rms (none with bath). **Bus:** No. 2 from Town Hall Square, or 13 from Central Station (just two stops away).

$ Rates (including breakfast): 325 Kr ($57) single; 435 Kr ($76.30) double, 125 Kr ($21.90) extra bed.

This simple but pleasant pension-style hotel represents another top value. The public hallways have old-fashioned lamps, mirrors, and chairs, while the large, comfortable rooms feature big windows and sinks. The shared baths are squeaky clean. Friendly owner/manager Brigitte Poulenard serves breakfast herself. Take the elevator to the third-floor reception. The hotel is a 10-minute walk from Town Hall.

3. DOUBLES FOR LESS THAN 500 KR ($87.70)

NEAR CENTRAL STATION

The hotels near Central Station are reasonably priced—by Copenhagen standards—offer clean, comfortable lodging with breakfast, and are well situated within walking distance of the city's major attractions, including Tivoli, Strøget, palaces, and museums, as well as the Tourist Office and the Scala Center. The area still attracts some transients, but don't let that put you off. (*Note:* For less than 500 Kr, don't expect a private bath.)

SAGA HOTEL, Colbjørnsensgade 20, DK-1625 København V. Tel. 31/24-49-44. Fax 31/24-60-33. 77 rms (13 with shower, sink, and toilet). **Directions:** One block from Central Station.

$ Rates (including breakfast): 275–380 Kr ($48.25–$66.65) single without bath; 420–580 Kr ($73.70–$101.75) with bath; 400–510 Kr ($70.20–$89.50) double without bath; 630–800 Kr ($110.50–140.35) with bath; Triples and quad are 200 Kr ($35.10) per person. ACCESS, AE, DC, EURO, MC, V.

FROMMER'S SMART TRAVELER: ACCOMMODATIONS

VALUE-CONSCIOUS TRAVELERS SHOULD TAKE ADVANTAGE OF THE FOLLOWING:

1. Private homes—recommended if you're on a tight budget.
2. Hotels that are immediately southwest of Central Station, along Colbjørnsensgade and Helgolandsgade (off Istedgade). Although many are above our price range, some offer excellent values. Note that this area is generally safe, but keep in mind it has its share of pornographic bookstores and attracts some "undesirables."

This perennial standby has long welcomed *Frommer* readers with comfortable rooms (6 singles, 53 doubles, 9 triples, 9 quads), a good breakfast, and a 5% discount. Rooms that have a bath also have a TV. The new owner/managers, Susanne and Søren Kaas (sister and brother) and Boye Birk, are young and extremely knowledgeable about Copenhagen and ways to save money here, and they are as accommodating as any hoteliers you'll find anywhere. The hotel has an inviting breakfast/dining room, where it serves a filling Danish supper Monday, Tuesday, and Wednesday for 38 Kr ($6.65); it also has a café and a bar.

MISSIONSHOTELLET NEBO, Istedgade 6, 1650 København V. Tel. 31/21-12-17. Fax 31/23-47-23 Telex 15284 DK. 97 rms (most with bath). TEL, TV **Directions:** A half block from Central Station.

$ Rates (including breakfast): May to mid-Sept 360–495 Kr ($63.15–$86.85) single without/with bath; 420–740 Kr ($73.70–$129.80) double without/with bath; mid-Sept to Apr prices fall 20% to 30%. ACCESS, AE, DC, EURO, MC, V.

The Nebo offers conventional budget rooms (43 singles and 54 doubles) with clock radios and tiny sinks, and most with phones. This is one of the three hotels in the area owned by the Danish Church; it is capably run by a friendly English-speaking staff. A few rooms are without TV, but guests are free to use the inviting hotel TV lounge. Breakfast is a traditional all-you-can-eat buffet served in a pretty room adjacent to a garden, where you may eat in summer.

NEAR THE CENTER

HOTEL CAPRIOLE, Frederiksberg Allé 7, 1621 København V. Tel. 31/21-64-64. Fax 33/25-64-60. 25 rms (4 with shower, sink, and toilet, 7 with shower only). **Bus:** No. 27 or 28 from Central Station (just two or three stops); walk if your luggage is light.

$ Rates (including breakfast): 300–350 Kr ($61.40–$81.90) single without/with shower; 400–525 Kr ($70.20–$92) double without/with shower.

This pretty four-story building adorned with faux classical columns is a 15-minute walk from Central Station. Plumbing in most rooms (5 singles, 20 doubles) is limited to sinks, though some are fitted with free-standing shower stalls and toilets, as well as a refrigerator. Windows are large, rooms in back are particularly quiet, and the bus stops half a block away. Owner Ellinor Plaugsoe will make you feel most welcome.

IBSENS HOTEL, Vendersgade 25, DK-1363 København K. Tel. 33/13-19-13. Fax 33/13-19-16. 49 rms (3 with shower, sink, and toilet). TEL TV **S-tog:** Nørreport.

$ Rates (including breakfast): 350 Kr ($61.40) single; 500 Kr ($87.70) double without bath, 600 Kr ($105.25) with shower only, 800–950 Kr ($140.35–$166.65) with bath and shower. ACCESS, AE, DC, EURO, MC, V.

Owned and managed by three women—Anni Kyær, Sine Manniche, and Helle Pedersen—Ibsens is a top choice because of its pretty interior, including a Victorian hallway, and excellent location. Huge antique wooden dressers and decorative cabinets are liberally dispersed throughout. Breakfast—an all-you-can-eat affair—is served in a homey dining room with tall windows. Honeymooners like Room 217. The reception area is on the second floor, and there is no elevator. Ørsteds Park and the Botanical Garden are nearby, and downtown is a 10-minute walk away.

FROMMER'S COOL FOR KIDS:

ACCOMMODATIONS

Hotel KFUM Soldaterhjem (see *page* 59) Kids won't mind that the decor is sparse. They'll go for the Ping Pong table in the café.

Saga Hotel (see *page* 63) The friendly, young owners make kids feel welcome (you might even get to meet Soren's gregarious young daughter, Camilla).

Ms. Gitte Kongstad (see *page* 67) This spacious lodging gives kids space to relax and play—Gitte's all for it. And breakfast is half price for small fry.

Peter and Lillian Pretzsch (see *page* 69) The garden out back as well as the proximity to two parks and the beach are real pluses.

Ms. Daphne Paladini (see *page* 70) With the beach and Bakken, the world's oldest amusement park, only a few minutes away—how can you miss?

Excelsior (see *page* 73) The prices may be for grown-ups but this hotel was made for children. How many places have a play area complete with Lego blocks in their lobby, or rooms with names like Rainbow and Parrot (with corresponding decor)?

4. ROOMS IN PRIVATE HOMES

Staying in a room in a private home has several advantages: low cost, a more intimate environment than a hotel but with privacy, and the opportunity to get to know a Danish host. All the hosts listed below are English-speaking and well traveled. There is also a strong network among hosts, and if one is booked, she will be able to direct you to another. Out of courtesy to hosts, always let them know when you plan to arrive so that you don't tie up their whole day or evening. (And be understanding if they cannot spend as much time socializing with you as you would like.) You'll be more than impressed with the lodging they provide and their sophistication as hosts. One even has a fax.

Use-It, in Huset, Rådhusstræde 13 (tel. 33/15-65-18), the alternative youth information office, rents about 40 private rooms for the lowest rates in town. Best of all, there's no commission charge. Moreover, private rooms listed here have proved to be every bit as suitable as the Central Station's more costly private accommodations. Rooms cost about 25 Kr ($21.95) for a single, 150 to 200 Kr ($26.35 to $35.00) for a double. From June 15 to September 14 the office is open daily from 9am to 7pm; the rest of the year, Monday through Friday only from 10am to 4pm.

Last but not least, you can contract a private room directly. Some of the best are listed below. Remember that each of these homes has only a handful of rooms available, so always call ahead to avoid disappointment.

IN THE CENTER

MS. TESSIE MEILING, Sølvgade 34b, 1307 København. Tel. 33/15-35-76 at home, **33/15-28-42** at work. 1 rm. **Bus:** No. 10 from Central Station to Kronprinsessegade, near the State Museum of Art.

$ Rates: Daily, 110 Kr ($19.30) single, 165 Kr ($28.95) double; weekly 550 Kr ($96.50) single, 770 Kr ($135.10) double.

Tessie Meiling, a kindergarten teacher, offers one of the city's best values for a stay of a week or more. Unfortunately there is only one room here, furnished with two single beds. The rates do not include breakfast, but you are more than welcome to use the kitchen to fix something for yourself.

Tessie's garret apartment—a three-story walk-up in a house built in 1845—has a country kitchen with wooden floors, cabinets, chests, and tables—all decorated by Tessie's artistic hand.

The shower is in the kitchen, but you have plenty of privacy. The entrance to the building is at the back of the courtyard.

MS. GITTE KONGSTAD, Skt. Annæ Gade 1b (4th Floor), 1416 København K. Tel. 31/57-24-66. Fax 31/57-24-86. 3 rms. **Bus:** No. 2 or 8 from City Hall; get off one stop after Knippels Bridge.

$ Rates: 175 Kr ($30.70) single; 250 Kr ($43.85) double; additional person, 75 Kr ($13.15). Breakfast with eggs costs 40 Kr ($7) extra, half price for kids.

Beam ceilings, hardwood floors, and lots of bookshelves and plants give this home a Scandinavian quaintness. The building—originally erected as an East India Trading Company warehouse in 1782—has been converted into condominium flats. Although the apartment is a fourth floor walk-up, the rooms are beautifully furnished and have a private entrance. TV, makeup mirror, and coffee- and cocoa-making facilities are added amenities. Guests particularly like chatting over breakfast. The outgoing host welcomes children and is quite knowledgeable about the city. The apartment is just 10 minutes from Copenhagen's busy shopping streets.

MS. TURID ARONSON, Brolæggerstræde 13. København. Tel. 33/14-31-46. 3 rms. **Bus:** No. 6 from Central Station to the canal.

$ Rates: 150 Kr ($26.30) single, 265 Kr ($46.50) double. Breakfast costs 30 Kr ($5.25).

The other private homes listed here may be more upscale, but none is more convenient than Ms. Aronson's—just one block from Strøget. Two of the three double rooms are adjacent to the tiled bathroom with a shower. The rooms are comfortable and guests have use of the kitchen; they may do their laundry here for 30 Kr ($5.25). Ms. Aronson sometimes rents bikes. Brolæggerstræde is a short street, only two blocks long. The Carlsberg Brewery was founded on it, at no. 5, in 1847.

MS. MARGRETHE KAÆ CHRISTENSEN, Amaliegade 26 (3rd Floor), 1256 København K. Tel. 33/13-68-61. 2 rms. **Bus:** No. 1 or 6 from Central Station to Amalienborg Palace.

$ Rates: 190 Kr ($33.35) single; 280 Kr ($49.15) double. A breakfast of bread, bacon, and eggs costs 40 Kr ($7) extra.

This is about as close as most of us will get to living at the royal Amalienborg Palace—just 50 yards away and directly across from the Italian Embassy. You'll be greeted by the exceedingly friendly and lively Ms. Christensen, whose elegant accommodations include a bath with tub and shower, as well as use of the kitchen. One room has a sink and double bed; the other has two single beds with a private entrance. Both have coffee-, tea-, and soup-making facilities.

IN FREDERIKSBERG

MS. BETTY WULFF, Jyllandsvej 24, 2000 Frederiksberg. Tel. 31/86-29-84. 3 rms. TV **Bus:** No. 1 from Central Station toward Frederiksberg to P. G. Ramms Allé.

$ Rate: 110 Kr ($19.30) per person.

The wood ceilings and walls make the rooms particularly cozy. Beds are fitted with Swedish health mattresses, and two of the rooms are linked together, making them ideal for families. Betty, a scientist with the World Health Organization who has worked at the Scripps Institute in La Jolla, Calif., serves free coffee and tea in the morning; you can buy pastries down the street. You're welcome to store cold food. If the house is full, ask about a room in her new house off Vesterbrogade, near Frederiksberg Park.

NILS AND ANNETTE HAUGBØLLE, Hoffmeyersvej 33, 2000 Frederiksberg. Tel. 31/74-87-87. 2 rms. **S-tog:** Line C to Peter Bangsvej, five stops from Central Station.

$ Rates: 100 or 150 Kr ($17.55 or $26.35) single; 230 Kr ($40.35) double.

Rooms in this charming two-story modern home are attractive, and one has a TV and balcony. The owners, a doctor and a nutritionist, live downstairs with their three children, away from the second-floor rented rooms. Check out their handy homemade reference file for tourists, complete with maps and brochures. The wood-and-tile bath has a tub and shower. Complimentary tea or coffee is available, and two bakeries and a Laundromat are nearby. The Haugbølles rent rooms June through mid-September only and prefer advance reservations.

GURLI AND VIGGO HANNIBAL, Folkets Allé 17, 2000 Frederiksberg. Tel. 31/86-13-10. 2 rms. **S-tog:** Peter Bangsvej (direction Ballerup).

$ Rates: 250 Kr ($43.85) per room; 80 Kr ($14) for an extra bed; single travelers may get a discount during the off-season. Breakfast costs 35 Kr ($6.15) per person extra.

This effervescent couple offers a memorable stay in their spotlessly clean house. Rooms here are modern, with blond-wood furniture and white cabinets. Room 12 features a private bath and a small anteroom with a hotplate for boiling water, but slightly smaller room 11 is equally inviting. The bath has a tub and shower, and the pipe-and-cork stairway and framed puzzles in the rooms are particularly unique. Guests are welcome to borrow from the home's small English-language library. If you call ahead, they may pick you up at the S-tog stop.

MS. HANNE LOYE, Ceresvej 1, 1863 Frederiksberg C. Tel. 31/24-30-27. 3 rms. **Bus:** 1 from Central Station; get off seven stops later in front of the Frederiksberg City Hall.

$ Rates: 300 Kr ($52.65) double; 150 Kr ($26.30) for an extra bed.

Antique furniture punctuates the pretty rooms on the second floor of this 60-year-old home. Ms. Loye, an actress, does not offer breakfast, but you'll find many stores nearby, including restaurants, bakeries, and a supermarket. Rooms are supplied with plates, cups, silverware, and glasses. You can luxuriate in the large tub and read one of the books in English that are scattered about. Two self-service laundries are within walking distance, and the house is only three blocks from the bus stop.

MS. ELSE SKØVBORG, Jyllandsvej 29, 2000 Frederiksberg. Tel. 31/46-25-72. 1 rm. **Bus:** No. 1 from Central Station toward Frederiksberg to P. G. Ramms Allé; then walk 3 blocks.

$ Rates: 300 Kr ($52.65) single or double.

Talkative, friendly, Ms. Skøvborg rents a single room with Danish cabinets and a collection of English books, just down the street from Ms. Wulff (see above). Guests are free to sit in the large back garden filled with apple trees. Ms. Skøvberg, an artist, and her husband designed the house. The only drawback is the tiny bath with shower only.

NORTH OF THE CENTER NEAR THE BEACH

PETER AND LILLIAN PRETZSCH, Christiansvej 36, 2920 Charlottenlund. Tel. 31/63-51-48. 4 rms. **S-tog:** Charlottenlund, about a 10-minute walk from the house.

$ Rates: 145 Kr ($24.45) single; 260 Kr ($45.60) double; 90 Kr ($15.80) for an extra bed. A full breakfast costs 40 Kr ($7), less for a modified breakfast.

Two double and two single rooms occupy the entire second floor of this pretty, quiet home, which is located near two parks. The bath has a separate tub and shower, and there are two toilets. Guests are free to enjoy the comfortable living room, pretty breakfast room, and large garden out back. The beach is a 25-minute walk away. Besides being a gracious host, Peter Pretzsch is a champion javelin thrower who has gone undefeated in Denmark for 17 years. If booking far in advance, send a deposit check in crowns for one night's lodging. The train ride to Charlottenlund takes 15 minutes.

MS. DAPHNE PALADINI, Dyrehavevej 20, 2930 Klampenborg. Tel. 31/64-07-44. 5 rms (none with bath). **S-tog:** Klampenborg.

$ Rates: 160 Kr ($28.10) single per person. Breakfast costs 45 Kr ($7.90).

Congenial Ms. Paladini, who is fluent in eight languages (she taught the queen Spanish), rents out three large double rooms and two singles. The two double rooms downstairs have a separate entrance and southern exposure. The bath, which features a tub, is the size of a studio apartment. Guests have access to a kitchen and barbecue, and the beach is a five-minute walk away. The train ride to Klampenborg takes 20 minutes; to get to the house, another three. Cross the street that fronts the station, then follow the street to your left and look for the white gate and white house set back from the street. Rooms are available April through December.

5. HOSTELS

Copenhagen has three International Youth Hostel Federation (IYHF) hostels, open to visitors of all ages. Unfortunately, they are not particularly well located (the two closest to downtown Copenhagen are listed here), but good transportation links and great rates counter this setback. Rates differ slightly from one hostel to the next, and preferential prices are given to IYHF cardholders. Sleeping bags are not permitted on the hostels' beds; you must supply your own sheet or rent one from reception for about 23 Kr ($4.05). IYHF cards can be purchased at any hostel.

OFFICIAL HOSTELS

BELLAHØJ VANDRERHJEM, Herbergvejn 8, 2700 København. Tel. 31/28-97-15. 308 beds. **Bus:** No. 2 from Town Hall Square; from the bus stop, walk to the corner, turn right, and follow Fuglsans Allé to the hostel.

$ Rates: 53 Kr ($9.30) per person with the IYHF card, 73 Kr ($12.80) without it. Breakfast costs 34 Kr ($5.95) extra; dinner, 54 Kr ($9.50). **Closed:** Nov 20–Dec 20.

Located in a residential area northwest of the city center and across from a park, Bellahøj has a large, pleasant lobby lounge, laundry facilities, a TV room, Ping-Pong room, vending machine, four showers for men and women on each floor, and lockers. There's no kitchen. The hostel is open 24 hours but rooms are off-limits from 10am to noon. The 30 rooms (a little on the dingy side) contain 4 to 14 beds each. Families pay 2 Kr (35¢) per person extra to have their own room. Allow 20 to 30 minutes' arrival time by bus from downtown Copenhagen.

COPENHAGEN HOSTEL, 55 Sjællandsbroen, 2300 København. Tel. 32/52-29-08. Fax 32/52-27-08. **Directions:** S-tog line C to Valby, then bus no. 37 toward Holmens Bro; or bus no. 46 from Central Station (6am to 6pm only).

$ Rates: 57 Kr ($10) per person with IYHF card, 77 Kr ($13.55) without it. Breakfast costs 34 Kr ($5.95) extra; dinner, 28, 34, or 54 Kr ($4.90, $5.95, or $9.50). **Closed:** Dec 20–Jan 2.

Renovations have made Copenhagen's oldest hostel a pretty nice place to locate. The house has no curfew, but its location—in the middle of a park more than 2 miles south of the city center—makes getting home after midnight difficult. In addition to 50 double and 87 quad rooms, there are laundry and cooking facilities, lockers, a Ping-Pong table, and a TV room. Check-in is from 1pm to after midnight, but call if you plan to arrive after 5 pm. Figure 30 to 45 minutes' travel time.

OTHER YOUTH CHOICES

Aside from Jørgensen Hotel, listed above, two other centrally located "unofficial" hostels are good picks for young Eurailers and hearty others.

COPENHAGEN SLEEP-IN, Per Henrik Lings Allé 6, 2100 København Ø. Tel. 31/26-50-59. 776 beds. **S-tog:** Nørdhavn. **Bus:** No. 1, 6, or 14 to Idrætsparken.

$ Rates (including breakfast): 75 Kr ($13.15) per person. **Open:** Late June–Aug.

Established by the government to alleviate tight tourist housing, the Copenhagen Sleep-in offers one of the cheapest places to sleep in the city. The four-bed rooms are only open in summer, and close during the day from noon to 4pm. The location, in Fælled Park, is not as inconvenient as the IYHF hostels, and the price includes breakfast, hot showers, and a guarded luggage-storage room. There are no kitchen facilities, and sleeping bags are required. No curfew.

VESTERBRO UNGDOMSGARD (City Hostel), Absalonsgade 8, 1658 København V. Tel. 31/31-20-70. 220 beds.

Directions: From Central Station, walk nine blocks along Istedgade to Absalonsgade.

$ Rates: 85–100 Kr ($15.45–$17.55) per person. Breakfast costs 25 Kr ($4.40) extra. **Open:** Early May–Aug.

Of Copenhagen's super-budget choices, this private hostel boasts the best location, within walking distance of Central Station. But this also makes it the most expensive of the lot. There are 5 to 10 beds in most rooms, plus a 60-bed dorm. Lockers and showers are included in the price.

6. OTHER SUPER-BUDGET CHOICES

CAMPING

As always, camping out is the cheapest accommodations option, though in Copenhagen it's only practical during the summer. Sites charge an average of 35 Kr ($6.15) per night. You'll also need a camping pass, which may be issued by any camp manager, is good for a year, and costs 24 Kr ($4.20) per person or 47 Kr ($9) per family.

A full list of legal spots is available from the tourist board, and **Bellahøj Camping,** Hvidkildevej, 2400 København NV (tel. 31/10-11-50), about 3 miles from the city center, is the closest campground. It's open June through August, daily from 7am to 10pm. Take bus no. 2 or 8 from Town Hall Square to the "Camping" stop. (And it's nice to know Bellahøj Hostel is nearby, in case of serious rain or a sudden cold snap.)

FARM & COUNTRY HOLIDAYS

It is possible to set up farm or country holidays in Denmark, where you either stay with a family and share breakfast or breakfast and supper with them, or rent a separate cottage on their property and do your own cooking. Rates are quite reasonable, starting at 150 Kr ($26.30) per person for a room with breakfast included; a house for four to six people for a week starts at 1,600 Kr ($280.70) in summer. For more information, contact the Danish Tourist Board.

7. LONG-TERM STAYS

If you plan on staying in Copenhagen for some time, visit the **Use-It** office in Huset (see "Rooms in Private Homes," above). They can help you with low-cost accommodations in either a student hall or a private apartment.

8. WORTH THE EXTRA BUCKS

HOTEL ABSALON, Helgolandsgade 15, 1653 København V. Tel. 31/24-22-11. Fax 31/24-34-11. Telex 19124 ABSLON DK. 260 rms (182 with bath). TEL TV **Directions:** Walk three blocks west from Central Station.

$ Rates (including breakfast): 400–735 Kr ($70.20–$128.95) single without/with bath; 500–900 Kr ($87.70–$157.90) double without/with bath. AE, DC, EURO, MC, V.

Electric sliding doors reveal the modern lobby and friendly reception of this first-class hotel. The Absalon looks a lot more expensive than you'd think. Rooms are well decorated, and fully equipped with trouser presses and hairdryers; rooms with bath also have TVs. Snack machines and laundry facilities are available 24 hours daily, and rates include an all-you-can-eat breakfast of Danish pastries, meats, cheeses, and more. In addition, there's a restaurant and bar on the premises. The Absalon has traditionally offered a special discount to Frommer readers—ask at the reception.

EXCELSIOR, Colbjørnsensgade 4, 1652 København. Tel. 31/24-50-85. Fax 31/24-50-87. Telex 15 550. 100 rms (most with bath with shower). MINIBAR TEL TV **Directions:** Two blocks from Central Station.

$ Rates: 375 Kr ($65.80) single without shower, 575 Kr ($100.90) double without shower, 525–650 Kr ($92.10–$114.05) single with shower, 770–865 Kr ($135.10–$151.75) double with shower.

This place wins as the most fun for kids, with bright colors throughout, a patio garden with swing and deck chairs, and a play area complete with Lego blocks in the lobby. Kids also love the theme rooms, with decor corresponding to the name on the door; favorites include Parrot, Rainbow, and Pyramid. Each room has a safe in it; some baths have tubs. Eight doubles and three singles have no bath.

CHAPTER 5

COPENHAGEN DINING

Smørrebrød, translated literally as "bread and butter," is Denmark's most famous culinary delicacy. These open-face sandwiches come in dozens of varieties, topped with everything from a single slice of cheese to mounds of sweet shrimp, and can be found almost everywhere. Even though it takes two or three servings to make a meal, you'll find that *smørrebrød* play an important part in the budget traveler's diet. Remember that *smørrebrød* are eaten with a knife and fork, and most of the shops that sell them are only open during the day.

Another Danish tradition is the buffet, or *smörgåsbord.* Typically, it begins with fish, then meat, cheese, fruit, and dessert, with a new plate provided for each course.

If you prefer à la carte, a popular, filling dish called *biksemad* consists of meat, potatoes, and onions. Danish beef and veal, which is quite good, is exported in large quantities. Lamb is available from May to September only.

Grov birkes are tasty nonsweet breakfast rolls (buy several and tuck them away for an impromptu picnic later in the day), and Danish pastries are rich and wonderful, no matter which you select (my *current* favorite is "Napoleon's Hat").

It is impossible to visit Copenhagen without sampling real "danish," and the best place to munch on this mouth-watering pastry and sip a piping hot cup of coffee, tea, or cocoa (all are popular here) is in a *conditori,* the elegant Danish equivalent of a café, pronounced *kon-DIT-ori.* The Danes often name their confections after famous people, such as princesses, actors, and queens. Take, for instance, the Margrethe cake, a chocolate cream and marzipan cake decorated with a daisy, a reference to Queen Margrethe's nickname (and the national flower).

No matter what you eat, however, you may wish to follow the Danish custom of drinking a cool pilsner beer and a shot of *aquavit*—a 90-proof potato-based schnapps. You'll have to resign yourself to expecting no free coffee refills; that's not the custom here.

1. MEALS FOR LESS THAN 45 KR ($7.90)

IN THE CENTER

KFUM SOLDATERHJEM CAFE, Gothersgade 115, second floor. Tel. 33/15-40-44.

Cuisine: FAST FOOD.

$ **Prices:** 15–38 Kr ($2.65–$6.65).

Open: Daily 10am–9:30pm.

A real find for low prices and pleasant, if a bit noisy, surroundings. You can order burgers, chicken, fish, salads, and even Danish hot meals. The dining room is pleasant and casual, the portions are ample, and the crowd is mostly well-scrubbed young men of the Royal Guard.

SABINES CAFETERIA, Teglgårdstræde 4. Tel. 33/12-82-71.

Cuisine: LIGHT FARE. **Directions:** Teglgårdstræde runs perpendicular to Nørre Voldgade, just south of Ørsteds Park.

$ **Prices:** 20–35 Kr ($3.55–$6.15).

Open: Mon–Fri 7:30am–2am, Sat 9am–1am, Sun noon–1am.

This small, undecorated café offers good light meals just off Nørre Voldgade. The morning breakfast special includes toast, honey, cheese, hard- or soft-boiled egg, yogurt, coffee, and juice or milk, and sells for just 35 Kr ($6.15). You can also get smoked salmon, paprika chicken, and smoked ham.

TOLDBOD BODEGA, Esplanaden 4. Tel. 33/12-93-31.

Cuisine: DANISH.

$ **Prices:** 20–50 Kr ($3.50–$8.80).

Open: Mon–Fri 10am–1am (kitchen closes at 8pm); Sat–Sun 10am–8pm.

A local favorite that tourists usually miss unless they saunter past it going to or from the Little Mermaid, it has a small bar, raspberry-colored tablecloths and napkins, and a particularly cozy corner table. Smørrebrød is a favorite on the menu.

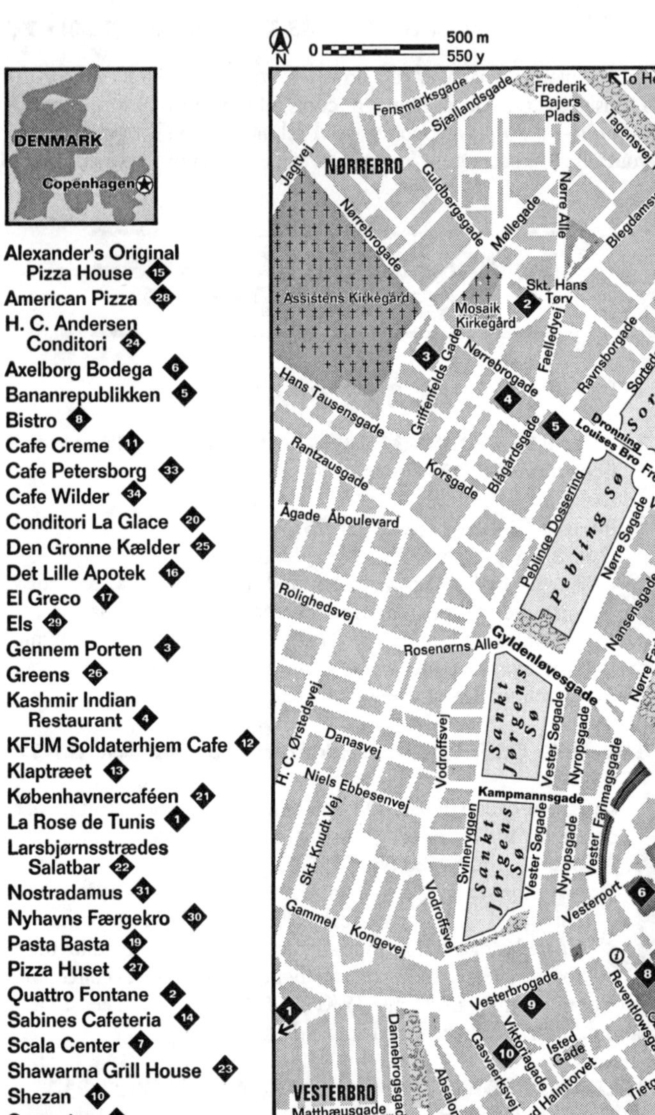

SHAWARMA GRILL HOUSE, Frederiksberggade 36. Tel. 33/12-63-23.

Cuisine: MIDDLE EASTERN.

$ Prices: 20–62 Kr ($3.55–$10.90).

Open: Daily 11am–11pm.

You will see a lot of these fast-food Middle Eastern places around the city, with almost identical menus and prices. This one has more

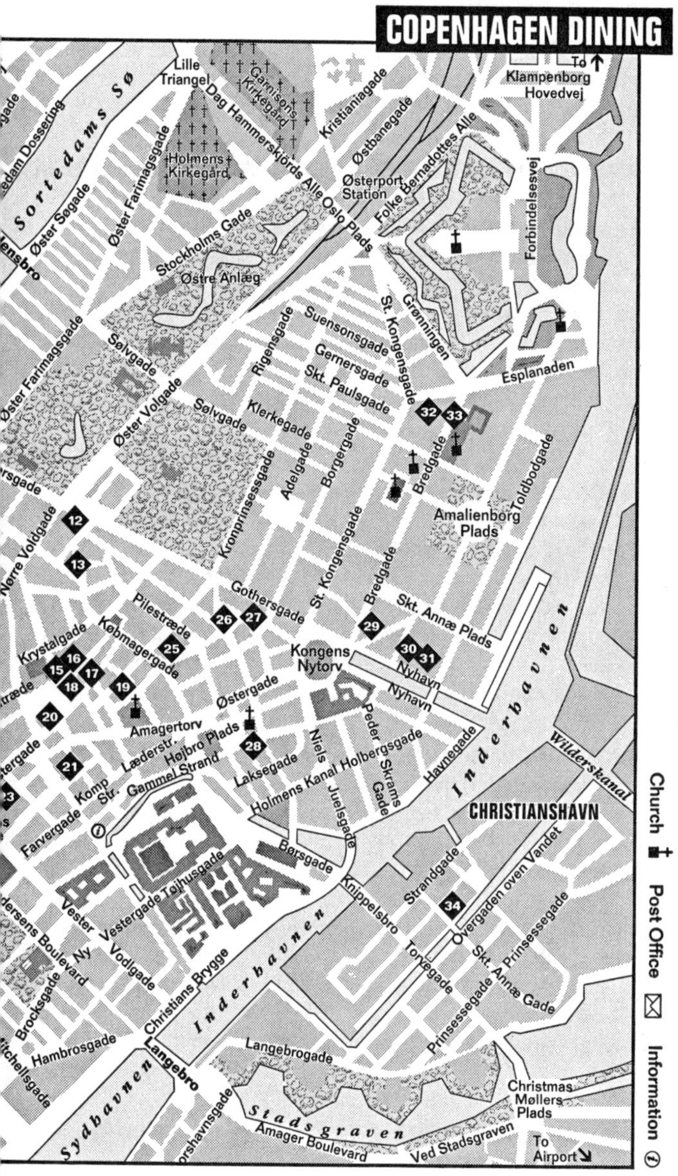

counter seating than most and is located just off Town Hall Square at the beginning of Strøget.

PIZZA HUSET, Gothersgade 21. Tel. 33/15-35-10.
Cuisine: ITALIAN.
$ Prices: 20–45 Kr ($3.55–$7.90).
Open: Daily 11am–6am.

Because of its late hours this take-out spot is a favorite with weekend night owls. Try the pizza sandwich, an oven-baked combination of ham, salad, and cheese.

LARSBJØRNSSTRÆDES SALATBAR, Larsbøkrnsstræde 7. Tel. 33/32-11-32.

Cuisine: LIGHT FARE. **Directions:** One block north of Frederiksberggade, near the Town Hall side of Strøget.

$ Prices: 22–30 Kr ($3.90–$5.25).

Open: Mon–Fri 10:30am–6:30pm.

Pastrami, deer, turkey, chicken, ham, salmon, and tuna are the most popular fillings at this tiny café. Some sandwiches are served on French bread. There's also fresh-squeezed orange, apple, and carrot juice, carrot cake, and all kinds of salads.

TH SØRENSEN, Vesterbrogade 15. Tel. 31/31-17-02.

Cuisine: DANISH.

$ Prices: 15–40 Kr ($2.65–$7).

Open: Mon–Fri 8am–8pm, Sat 10am–6pm.

Located on the main street, just west of Central Station, this shop's copious mouth-watering window display will stop you in your tracks. No need to worry about reading the menu—just point, pay, and enjoy! You may also get salad and American-style heroes.

KLAPTRÆET, Kultorvet 11. Tel. 33/13-00-09.

Cuisine: LIGHT FARE. **Directions:** Kultorvet is a traffic-free pedestrian square, two blocks southeast of Nørreport Station.

$ Prices: 24–42 Kr ($4.21–$7.37).

Open: Mon–Wed 9am–2am, Thurs 9am–3am, Fri–Sat 10am–3am, Sun 11:30am–midnight.

Downstairs from an alternative movie house, this bohemian café serves cheap breakfasts, lunches, and light meals to students, travelers, and assorted others. Chili con carne, salads, soups, and sandwiches are among the offerings. Old movie posters and newspapers double as wallpaper. Order and pay at the bar; they'll bring your food.

DEN GRONNE KÆLDER (The Green Cellar), Klareboderne 10. Tel. 33/15-21-81.

Cuisine: VEGETARIAN.

$ Prices: 28–35 Kr ($4.90–$6.15).

Open: Mon–Fri 11am–6:30pm, Sat 11am–2pm.

Small and to the point, it's got six tables or take-out service. Main courses such as quiche, pizza, or lasagne, come with salad. If salad is your main course, there are half a dozen from which to choose, along with soup and fruit or vegetable juices.

SCALA CENTER, Scala Axeltorv 2. Tel. 33/15-12-15.

Cuisine: INTERNATIONAL.

$ Prices: 26–52 Kr ($4.55–$9.10).

Open: Daily 7am–1am or 2am.

Located across from the main entrance to Tivoli, with an entrance on Vesterbrogade, this sparkling center of activity houses a good variety of fast-food stands adjacent to more expensive cafés and international restaurants. Pizza, pasta, smørrebrød, chicken, quiche, hamburgers, and other favorites are all available at moderate prices. Communal tables mean that you can satisfy everyone and still eat together. Scala's ground level features bargain eateries, tops among them **Streckess, Shawarma Scala,** and a popular **gelati counter.** Its third floor is home to more expensive sit-down places you can check out.

NEAR THE CENTER

BANANREPUBLIKKEN, Nørrebrogade 13. Tel. 31/39-79-21.

Cuisine: INTERNATIONAL.

$ Prices: Lunch 22–42 Kr ($3.85–$7.35); dinner 60–100 Kr ($10.50–$17.55).

Open: Daily 11am–2am; lunch 11:30am–4pm, dinner 6–10pm.

Not to be confused with the trendy safari clothing store, this is a rustic café with a blackboard menu featuring salads, sandwiches, guacamole, and homemade cakes. African and Latin American dishes are served at dinner. Live bands perform Latin music and reggae here several nights a week; there's a 40 Kr ($7) cover on Thursday and Saturday; free admission on Tuesday, but the price of beer goes up 4 Kr (70¢).

2. MEALS FOR LESS THAN 60 KR ($10.50)

IN THE CENTER

RESTAURANT SPORVEJEN, Gråbrødre Torv 17. Tel. 33/13-31-01.

Cuisine: AMERICAN.

$ **Prices:** 29–69 Kr ($5.10–$12.15). Cash only.
Open: Daily 11am–midnight.

Located in an authentic old tram car, which is itself inside a building, Sporvejen's "tin-can" interior is reminiscent of an American diner. The chef, cooking on a small grill near the front door, dishes your dinners right onto the plate in front of you. Specialties include hamburgers and omelets.

AMERICAN PIZZA, Vingardestræde 21 at Nikolaj Plads. Tel. 33/12-55-97.
Cuisine: ITALIAN.
$ **Prices:** All-you-can-eat for 49 Kr ($8.60). DC, EURO, MC, V.
Open: Daily noon–11pm.

"This place encourages pig-outs," claims vivacious hostess Prescilla Neri, originally from the Philippines. That it does, with a large, fresh salad bar and assorted pizzas that include ham, pepperoni, and ground beef. Request vegetarian or deep-dish varieties. The decor includes red tablecloths and a large poster of the Brooklyn Bridge;

FROMMER'S SMART TRAVELER: RESTAURANTS

1. Go ethnic. The city has myriad possibilities, with prices for the budget-minded. (A Danish friend suggests if you order a step above the lowest item on the menu, what you get is gourmet.)
2. Look for those small, inconspicuous places off the beaten path, such as along the side streets branching off Strøget; those around Gråbrødre Torv, two blocks north of Strøget; and those clustered around Vesterbrogade, north of Central Station.
3. Make lunch your main meal rather than dinner. Midday prices tend to be lower, and restaurants offer daily specials.
4. Eat outside if the weather's good. Grab a sandwich or some picnic rations and find a welcoming bench along Strøget. You're likely to get free entertainment along with your meal.
5. Indulge yourself at an all-you-can-eat pizza buffet. The city has several.
6. Sample a Danish smörgåsbord. They're not cheap but offer terrific value for the quality and quantity of the food.
7. Ease up on booze; it's heavily taxed and adds substantially to the cost of the meal.

music by Johnny Mathis or Crystal Gale is likely to be playing in the background.

NOSTRADAMUS, Nyhavn 31. Tel. 33/14-52-44.
Cuisine: ITALIAN.
$ Prices: 49–93 Kr ($8.60–$16.30). AE, EURO, MC, V.
Open: Daily 11am–midnight.

It's a restaurant, steak house, and pizzeria rolled into one, and you'll do fine price-wise if you stick to the pasta and pizza dishes. Relaxed and cozy, it features exposed beams and brick walls, two dining levels, and a striking glass facade.

ALEXANDER'S ORIGINAL PIZZA HOUSE, Lille Kannikestræde 5. Tel. 33/12-55-36.
Cuisine: PIZZA.
$ Prices: Pizza and salad buffet 55 Kr ($9.65). AE, DC, EURO, MC, V.
Open: Daily noon–midnight.

Only pizza and salad are on the menu here, and Alexander's best deal is the self-service all-you-can-eat buffet. Since most of the pizzas on the menu are offered at the buffet (along with a copious salad bar), only the pickiest eaters should order à la carte. The restaurant's dark, wood interior, complete with an upright piano, old beer barrels, and wagon wheel, is reminiscent of a saloon from America's Old West. Evenings from 6pm to 8pm get busy, as an eternal line surrounds the serving area.

KØBENHAVNER CAFÉEN (Copenhagener Café), Badstuestræde 10. Tel. 33/32-80-81.
Cuisine: DANISH.
$ Prices: Daily special with five items 59 Kr ($10.35); daily special with seven items 89 Kr ($15.60); main courses 35–58 Kr ($6.15–$10.20). DC, EURO, MC, V.
Open: Daily 10am–midnight; kitchen 11:30am–10pm.

Only half a block from Strøget, yet seemingly miles from the hustle and modernity outside. The menu comes with an English translation, and you won't leave hungry. The daily special features herring, fried filet of fish, roast pork, and bread; the deluxe version adds roast beef, Danish meatballs, chicken, salad, and cheese. The small café fills up with customers and easy conversation, and it can get smoky. There's free piano music Thursday through Saturday from 9:30pm to 2am and Sunday from 4 to 7pm.

NEAR THE CENTER

CAFE WILDER, Wildersgade 56 and Sankt Annæ Gade, Christianshavn. Tel. 31/54-71-83.

Cuisine: LIGHT FARE. **Bus:** No. 2 one stop into Christianshavn.
$ **Prices:** 18–80 Kr ($3.15–$14). EURO, MC, V.
Open: Mon–Fri 9am–2am, Sat–Sun noon–2am.

This corner café offers everything from soup and sandwiches to cold salads like chicken pesto to hot dishes (served from 6:30 to 9:30pm only). It attracts all ages, including young parents with a baby carriage in tow. The daily fare is displayed in the counter.

RESTAURANT SHEZAN, Victoriagade 22, at the corner of Istedgade. Tel. 31/24-78-88.

Cuisine: PAKISTANI.
$ **Prices:** 32–65 Kr ($5.65–$11.40). Cash only.
Open: Daily 11am–11pm.

One of the cheapest sit-down restaurants in town, Shezan serves good Pakistani food that doesn't spare the spices. Arched windows, columned table dividers, and a clientele made up primarily of Pakistani diners faithfully reproduce the feeling of the Asian subcontinent. Pick up your food either with a fork or Pakistani style (with the bread served with your main course). Specialties include spicy lamb, chicken, beef, and curry dishes. Look for the blue-and-white facade.

QUATTRO FONTANE, Guldbergsgade 3. Tel. 31/39-49-41.

Cuisine: ITALIAN. **Bus:** No. 5 or 16 along Nørrebrogade to Elmergade and walk one block north.
$ **Prices:** 36–72 Kr ($6.35–$12.65). Cash only.
Open: Daily 4–midnight.

Despite its decor including hanging wax grapes, chianti bottles, and boot-shaped map, this place is really popular. Mid-priced meat and fish dishes are available, or stick to their well-priced pasta and pizza, both made fresh on the premises. Ask about the daily special. The restaurant is well worth the bus ride from the city center. Reservations are not accepted.

KASHMIR INDIAN RESTAURANT, Nørrebrogade 35. Tel. 35/37-54-71.

Cuisine: INDIAN. **Reservations:** Recommended at dinner. **Bus:** No. 7 from Town Hall, or 16 from Town Hall or Central Station, to Nørrebrogade in the Nørrebro area of town.
$ **Prices:** 45–98 Kr ($7.90–$17.20). AE, DC, EURO, MC, V.
Open: Lunch daily 11am–3pm; dinner daily 3–11pm.

Excellent food is served in an authentic Indian environment, sitar music and all. And although owner Mohan Bains boasts that he has served the Queen of Denmark, it's the locals who keep him in business—they come in droves. The lunch special changes daily, but always includes a main course, rice, bread, and salad.

3. MEALS FOR LESS THAN 80 KR ($14.05)

IN THE CENTER

AXELBORG BODEGA, Axeltorv 1. Tel. 33/11-00-96.

Cuisine: DANISH.

$ Prices: 35–110 Kr ($6.15–$19). AE, DC, EURO, MC, V.

Open: Sun–Thurs 10am–1am; Fri–Sat 10am–2pm. The kitchen closes at 9:30pm; the lunch special is served 11am–5pm.

Considering that the Benneweis Circus is across the street, it seems appropriate that this place is loud. The tavern's clientele joke with one another while downing beers the whole time. The Danes use the word *bodega* to refer to a "local bar." The menu at this one features ham and eggs and omelets for lunch; and roast beef, fried fish, pork chops, and veal for dinner, which will cost about $10 when you order with care.

GREENS, Grønegade 12–14. Tel. 33/15-16-90.

Cuisine: VEGETARIAN.

$ Prices: 42–129 Kr ($7.40–$22.65); all-you-can-eat lunch salad buffet 65 Kr ($11.40); Saturday dinner buffet 98 Kr ($17.20). EURO, MC, V.

Open: Lunch Mon–Sat 11:30am–5pm; dinner Mon–Thurs 5:30–9pm.

This vegetarian restaurant serves up attractive, healthful food in an equally pretty, smoke-free environment. Several different rooms are all united by comfortable furnishings, wood floors, and pretty potted plants. The all-you-can-eat self-service lunch is more filling and significantly less expensive than the more formal dinner. And orders to go are even cheaper than eating in. During the summer, try their other restaurant, in Tivoli behind the fountain and to the left of the concert hall.

EL GRECO, Skindergade 20. Tel. 33/32-93-44.

Cuisine: GREEK. **Reservations:** Suggested Thurs–Sat nights.

$ Prices: All-you-can-eat buffet 54 Kr ($9.50) 11:30am–4pm; 79 Kr ($13.90) in the evening. AE, DC, EURO, MC, V.

Open: Daily 11:30am–11:30pm (last orders at 11pm).

Amid white stucco walls, wood-beamed ceilings, and Mediterranean farmhouse decor, you may enjoy a large "Greek smorgasbord" with more than 20 hot main courses. Help yourself to meats, fish, chicken, rice, potatoes, and other specially prepared Greek foods; and eat as much as you like. This popular restaurant is well situated; choose a seat upstairs.

PASTA BASTA, Valkendorfsgade 22. Tel. 33/11-21-31.

Cuisine: ITALIAN.

$ Prices: 55–198 Kr ($9.65–$34.75); Pasta Basta table 69 Kr ($12.10). ACCESS, DC, EURO, MC, V.

Open: Daily 11:30am–5am.

Except for its name, Pasta Basta has everything going for it: a tastefully decorated, modern interior, large windows overlooking a romantic cobblestone street, and an all-you-can-eat buffet with top-notch food. For reasons unexplained, some diners order a hot pasta dish in addition to the Pasta Basta table. Help yourself to the house wine that's automatically placed on each table. Measuring stripes down the side mean that you only pay for as much as you drink. The restaurant is located near Strøget, behind Holy Ghost Church.

BISTRO, in Central Station. Tel. 33/14-12-32.

Cuisine: DANISH.

$ Prices: Salad buffet 56 Kr ($9.82); fish or cheese buffets 46 or 68 Kr ($8.10 or $11.90); lunch specials 33–47 Kr ($5.80–$8.25); daily specials (served all day) 48–59 Kr ($8.40–$10.35); main courses 70–110 Kr ($12.30–$19.30), with complimentary salad buffet, half price for kids under 16 who get the same dish as their parents; cold Danish buffet 115 Kr ($20.20). ACCESS, AE, DC, EURO, MC, V.

Open: Daily 11:30am–10pm.

If you think an outstanding restaurant in a train station is an oxymoron, you're in for a pleasant surprise. At the elegant, airy Bistro, with its columns, arched ceiling, and lights resembling hanging artichokes, choose from several buffets (the restaurant is best known for its cold buffet, priced above budget but worth the splurge). You may also order à la carte. Menu offerings include roast beef or pork, turkey, duck, halibut steamed in white wine, and grilled salmon. On Sunday, a special three-course family dinner costs only 79 Kr ($13.85).

CAFE PETERSBORG, Bredgade 76. Tel. 33/12-50-16.

Cuisine: DANISH.

$ Prices: Daily lunch and dinner specials, 60–70 Kr ($10.50–$12.30); combination platters, 80 and 90 Kr ($14 and $15.80); à la carte, 50–110 Kr ($8.80–$19.30).

Open: Daily noon–10:30pm.

A pretty place, it has dark wood paneling and furniture, exposed beams, three dining areas, and candles and flowers on the tables. The extensive menu features filling Danish meals, but you can get a sandwich at lunch (a good possibility after visiting the Little Mermaid, which is nearby). Prices are reasonable for alcohol. It can get smoky when crowded.

DET LILLE APOTEK, Store Kannikestræde 15. Tel. 33/12-56-06.

Cuisine: DANISH.

$ Prices: House plate 59 and 79 Kr ($10.35 and $13.85); dinner 98–125 Kr ($17.20–$21.90). ACCESS, AE, DC, EURO, V.

Open: Daily, lunch 11am–5pm, dinner 5:30–11pm.

This corner restaurant with its brick floor, low ceilings, and three small dining areas has been here since 1720. The hanging lamps have been electrified but not much else has changed, including the hearty Danish fare they serve. The name means "The Little Chemist," which is what it used to be. It's opposite Alexander's Pizza, and a block west of Købmagergade.

4. MEALS FOR LESS THAN 110 KR ($19.30)

IN THE CENTER

NYHAVNS FÆRGEKRO, Nyhavn 5. Tel. 33/15-15-88.

Cuisine: DANISH.

$ Prices: Herring buffet with 15 choices 62 Kr ($10.90); single-choice herring 29 Kr ($5.10); main courses 125–135 Kr ($21.90–$23.70); smørrebrød 19–53 Kr ($3.35–$9.30).

Open: Daily 11:30am–11:30pm.

This place is unique for two reasons: It serves French champagne by the glass, and it offers a decadent, delectable *desserts-only* buffet featuring such temptations as white chocolate mousse, profiterole, and a tart of the day. The champagne costs 29 Kr ($5.10) a glass; there are unlimited visits to the dessert table for 67 Kr ($11.75). Less indulgent fare for the strong-willed includes 15 different open-face sandwiches and *biksemad,* a traditional dish with beef, potatoes, and egg. The restaurant itself is striking, with a black-and-white marble floor, spiral stairway from an old streetcar, and unique lights that serve as call buttons for the waitresses.

NEAR THE CENTER

GENNEM PORTEN, Griffenfeldtsgade 7A. Tel. 31/35-12-05.

Cuisine: VEGETARIAN. **Reservations:** Recommended for dinner.

$ Prices: Buffet lunch 59 Kr ($10.80); 3-course lunch 95 Kr ($16.65); buffet dinner 89 Kr ($15.60); 3-course dinner 145 Kr ($25.45). A la carte dishes run about 80 Kr ($14) each.

Open: Sun noon–2:30pm (lunch only), Tues–Sat noon–2:30pm and 7:30–9:30pm. **Bus:** No. 5, 7, or 16.

Opened in 1990 to rave reviews, this pretty vegetarian restaurant is decorated with Danish artwork and furniture. It has a tile floor, bright white walls, and oval windows in parentheses of country curtains. The glass-enclosed smoking area makes a strong social statement. The food is startlingly fresh, most of it organically grown. The restaurant is in a holistic center that sponsors workshops related to the body, mind, and spirit; a meal here is an experience for all three.

LA ROSE DE TUNIS, Vesterbrogade 120. Tel. 31/24-06-51.

Cuisine: TUNISIAN/FRENCH. **Reservations:** Recommended on weekends. **Bus:** No. 6 from Central Station to the fourth stop.

$ Prices: 80–145 Kr ($14.05–$25.45). AE, DC, EURO, MC, V.

Open: Daily 5–10pm.

Uneven whitewashed walls, tile mosaics, handwoven rugs, and traditional music mimic an upper-class Tunisian home. Co-owner Moktar Redjeb directs an excellent kitchen, and although dishes are not cheap, the food is terrific. Try the brik (thin, crisp pancakes stuffed with tuna, chicken, or meat), or the couscous (pastina made of grain flour topped with meats and/or vegetables). This restaurant, with flowers, candles, and white linen tablecloths, provides an elegant night out.

FOR DESSERT

Just look at all the delicious bakeries around Copenhagen and you'll understand why Denmark's pastries are world famous. Don't ask for a danish, though. Just point to the dessert that catches your fancy.

CONDITORI LA GLACE, Skoubogade 3–5. Tel. 33/14-46-46.

Cuisine: DESSERT.

$ Prices: Cakes 6.50–16 Kr ($1.15–$2.80); coffee or hot chocolate 22 Kr ($3.90).

Open: Mon–Fri 8am–6pm (last serving at 5:30pm), Sat 8:30am–6pm, Sun 10am–6pm.

Founded in 1870, this dignified café maintains the elegance of a bygone era. Order at the counter and take a seat. When your food is ready, it's brought to your table. Real dessert lovers should try "Sports Cake," the house specialty; these whipped cream–topped caramel cream puffs are rivaled in richness only by the café's ultra-chocolaty hot cocoa. Skoubogade is a small street off Strøget.

Since 1989, there has been a new, equally elegant and popular La Glace at Kongens Nytorv 2 at Bredgade (tel. 33/14-46-46). It's in a five-story, 370-year-old house with a view of the square and Nyhavn.

H. C. ANDERSEN CONDITORI, in Rådhusarkaden, H. C. Andersens Blvd. and Vesterbrogade. Tel. 33/32-80-98.
Cuisine: DESSERT.
$ Prices: 12–18 Kr ($2.10–$3.15).
Open: Mon–Sat 8am–6pm, Sun 1–5pm.

Everything from the pastries to the ice-cream sundaes looks enticing in this bright spot. Tip your hat to the near-life-size, 139-kilogram (306-pound) marzipan replica of Mr. Andersen at the door. There's also a painting of the author. Seating is inside and in the mall—a great spot for people watching.

CAFE CREME, Vendersgade 5. Tel. 33/93-29-00.
Cuisine: DESSERT/SNACKS.
$ Prices: 34–40 Kr ($5.95–$7). Cash only.
Open: Mon–Fri 8am–8pm, Sat–Sun 8am–10pm.

Compared to the other two listings, this is an unassuming, nontouristic kind of place, mentioned here for just that reason. (The desserts are better in the other two.) But here you'll see friends meeting over a cup of coffee or a glass of wine and young families dropping by during a day's outing. It's nice to sit in the midst of them. Best on the blackboard menu are the coffees, everything from espresso to café crème to Irish. Besides desserts, you can get short-order meals. Order at the counter and bus your own table.

5. SPECIALTY DINING

LOCAL BUDGET BETS/FAVORITE MEALS

Anytime you walk into noisy **Axelborg Bodega,** Axeltorv 1 (tel. 33/11-00-96), you'll find it filled with locals—better said, regulars; the camaraderie can't be beat, and the varied menu's good, too. **Klaptræet,** Kultorvet 11 (tel. 33/13-00-00), is a favorite student hangout, definitely a bohemian place. After dining on their light fare, you may want to take in an avant-garde film at the theater upstairs. A somewhat older (and definitely livelier) crowd goes to **Københavner Caféen (Copenhagener Café),** Badstuestræde 10 (tel. 33/32-80-81), just off Strøget, to dine on hearty Danish platters and enjoy piano music and easy conversation.

Copenhageners always recommend **Ida Davidsen,** at Store Kongensgade 70 (tel. 31/91-36-55), for smørrebrød. Though it is hardly a budget place, it's mentioned here for its uniqueness and quality. If you happen to pass by or decide to splurge, peruse the famous menu that's so long it's in the *Guinness Book of World Records*. Ida is a real person, and she inherited her knack for working with foods from her parents and famous grandfather, Oskar Davidsen, who built the family reputation.

FAST FOOD

It's readily available along **Strøget** and **Vesterbrogade,** in **Tivoli,** and in the **Scala** shopping/dining/entertainment complex and **Central Station,** both with entrances on Vesterbrogade.

DANISH BUFFET

Dine from heaving buffet tables under vaulted ceilings in the **Bistro,** in Central Station (tel. 33/14-12-32). Danes often go there, but visitors to Copenhagen rarely get beyond the short-order places in the train station.

DINING COMPLEX

Scala, Scala Axeltorv 2 (tel. 33/15-12-15), also with an entrance on Vesterbrogade, has several levels of eateries, with escalators and glass-enclosed elevators connecting them. The most inexpensive places (and a counter selling good, but not cheap, ice cream) are on the ground floor.

BREAKFAST

The buffet breakfasts served in hotels are sumptuous, filling, and good deals. If you like take-out (also affordable), head for **Arkade Konditoriet,** in City Arkaden on Strøget, at Østergade 32–34, at the corner of Kristen Bernikows Gade (tel. 33/13-78-16), for pastries and breads. It opens at 8am (noon on Sunday). Brunch is not a big tradition in Copenhagen, but you can find it occasionally.

AFTERNOON TEA

The hands-down favorite for teatime for the past century or so has been **Conditori La Glace,** just off Strøget at Skoubogade 3–5 (tel. 33/14-46-46). Don't wait too late to go; they're *supposed* to close at 6pm, but I've found the doors closed earlier on more than one occasion. In 1989 La Glace opened a second café (same name) in a

FROMMER'S COOL FOR KIDS: RESTAURANTS

Sporvejen (pronounced *Spore-vine*) (*see p. 79*) It's housed in an old tram car, and kids can munch on hamburgers or omelets and pretend they're taking a trip.

American Pizza (*see p. 80*) If you don't see your favorite kind of pizza, just ask. The chef is very accommodating, and kids like the easygoing atmosphere.

Bistro (*see p. 84*) More upscale, this restaurant is equally welcoming to young folks. It offers them a half price meal if they order the same dish as their parents.

five-story, 370-year-old house at Kongens Nytorv 2. Both conditories get crowded, so if you want more space and quicker service (but less ambience), head to **H. C. Andersen Conditori,** in Rådhusarkaden on H. C. Andersen Boulevard, opposite Town Hall. It's a great place to people-watch. All three places open at 8am, later on Saturday; only the Kongens Nytorv La Glace is open on Sunday. **Arkade Konditoriet** (see "Breakfast," above) serves a teatime special daily.

LATE NIGHT/24-HOUR

Open the longest, latest hours of any place in Copenhagen, this one is purely take-out and you have to like pizza to take advantage of it. It's **Pizza Huset,** Gothersgade 21 (tel. 33/15-35-10), serving daily from 11am to 6am.

PICNIC FARE AND WHERE TO EAT IT

Aldi and **Netto** are two popular supermarket chains. Other markets such as **Irma** and **Brugsen** usually have more extensive selections but are often more expensive.

A conveniently located market is in the back of **City Arkaden** on Strøget at Østergade 32–34. Gather some goodies, then take your picnic onto Strøget or to nearby Kongens Nytorv for an unhurried meal. If you prefer a more natural setting for outdoor dining, the ramparts around the Kastellet, near the Little Mermaid, are a green and peaceful spot.

6. WORTH THE EXTRA BUCKS

ELS, Store Strandstræde 3. Tel. 31/14-13-41.

Cuisine: DANISH. **Reservations:** Recommended.

$ Prices: Quick lunch with herring, salmon, meat, and cheese 98 Kr ($17.20); main course at lunch 128 Kr ($22.45); 2-course lunch 152 Kr ($26.65); 3-course lunch 176 Kr ($30.90); 2-course dinner 176 Kr ($30.90); 3-course dinner 214 Kr ($37.55). AE, DC, EURO, MC, V.

Open: Daily, lunch 11:30am–3pm, dinner 5:30pm–1am.

Visually and culinarily memorable, Els is also outstanding for location (near Kongens Nytorv), atmosphere, and romance. The original decor dates from 1853, with six murals of women depicting the four seasons and the twin muses of dance and music. The prix-fixe menu changes daily (the lunchtime smörgåsbord monthly), ensuring the freshest foods available. At dinner, expect dishes such as duck liver pâté, caviar, crab bisque, pheasant, and filet of sole. The last dinner orders are taken at 10pm.

CHAPTER 6

WHAT TO SEE & DO IN COPENHAGEN

Copenhagen is wonderfully diverse when it comes to activities and exercise options. Choose from museums, castle tours, and boat rides through the canals—Amsterdam has nothing on Copenhagen. While strolling the streets, you'll see unique architecture. Or bike around the city like the Danes—and on free bikes, too. And don't forget to see the Little Mermaid; she's small but not to be missed.

SUGGESTED ITINERARIES

IF YOU HAVE 1 DAY

Day 1 If this is your first visit, and you're a walker, as I am, devote the entire day to getting to know this very walkable city on foot. Explore every block of **Strøget,** the world's longest pedestrian street, and the smaller pedestrian walkways branching off it to the north. And don't overlook **Nyhavn,** the old sailors' quarter, across Kongens Nytorv from the east end of Strøget (walking tour nos. 1 and 2 will lead the way).

If this is not your first visit, or you prefer to be indoors rather than out, head over to 17th-century **Rosenborg Castle** to see the opulent royal interiors and the crown jewels (the castle itself is one). After lunch (a picnic on the castle grounds, perhaps), visit the **State Museum of Fine Art,** the largest in Denmark and conveniently within walking distance of Rosenborg Castle.

Save the evening for **Tivoli,** to Denmark what Disneyland is to the United States.

DID YOU KNOW . . . ?

- Denmark is the smallest country in Scandinavia, but Copenhagen, with half a million inhabitants, is the second-largest city.
- Denmark has the highest standard of living of any EC country.
- Three-quarters of Denmark's land area is devoted to agriculture.
- Denmark has no mountains or rivers and on average it is only 98 feet above sea level.
- In 1972, Queen Margrethe became the first female monarch in Denmark's history.
- Only 53 Danish Jews lost their lives in World War II, due to an enormous national effort to save them.
- The Danes love candles and burn them even at breakfast.
- The average Danish family has 1.2 kids and 5 bikes.
- 90% of the Danes own their own homes.
- The legal requirement for marriage in Copenhagen is one week's residency.
- Denmark is the world's largest exporter of insulin and windmills.

IF YOU HAVE 2 DAYS

Day 1 Spend the first day as outlined above.

Day 2 Spend the morning at the *Little Mermaid* and nearby **Churchill Park** and **Fight for Freedom Museum.** Try to make it to **Amalienborg Palace** by noon for the changing of the guard. Back in the city center in the afternoon, walk down to **Gammel Strand** to see the statues of Bishop Absalon and the Fisherwoman, climb the **Round Tower** for a fine view of Copenhagen, and visit the **Ny Carlsberg Glyptotek** to see the ancient sculptures and the French and Danish modern art and, within walking distance, **Christiansborg Castle** for the queen's reception rooms and the foundation, which dates from Bishop Absalon's time.

IF YOU HAVE 3 DAYS

Days 1–2 Spend the first two days as outlined above.

Day 3 Take the train to **Louisiana,** one of the world's great modern art museums and not to be missed. The grounds, filled with priceless sculpture, overlook the Danish coast.

IF YOU HAVE 5 DAYS OR MORE

Days 1–3 Spend the first three days as outlined above.

Day 4 Take a **brewery tour,** and enjoy the free samples, or visit the lovely **Botanical Gardens** north of Nørreport. If your curiosity is piqued, venture into **Christiania,** the city's experimental community in Christianshavn. While on the island, be sure to see the **Church of Our Savior** and its unusual spire. In the evening, enjoy **jazz** in one or more of the city's lively clubs.

Day 5 This is castle country, so experience one or two of the biggies: **Kronborg** (the setting for Shakespeare's *Hamlet*), in Helsingør, and **Frederiksborg,** in Hillerød, both in North Zealand. Back in Copenhagen, visit the centrally located **National Museum** and do some souvenir hunting in its well-stocked shop.

1. THE TOP ATTRACTIONS

TIVOLI, Vesterbrogade 3. Tel. 33/15-10-01.

When Tivoli opened in 1843, the park was well outside the city center. Today, of course, it is Copenhagen's centerpiece, attracting more than 4.5 million visitors annually. And although the grounds are full of white-knuckle rides, few would relegate Tivoli to the category of "amusement park." Tivoli is an integral part of Copenhagen, and is the city's main showcase for Danish culture, music, and entertainment. Every day brings with it a full program of open-air concerts, cabaret theater, dancing, pantomime, and other special events. Most are free or fairly priced. And there are the visual effects of 20 acres filled with Turkish and Oriental architecture and 110,000 shimmering lights.

The majority of the performances are staged at night, when the park takes on truly magical proportions. Thousands of lights shimmer through the trees, and every Wednesday, Friday, Saturday, and Sunday night fireworks light the sky with a cavalcade of color. Don't overlook an afternoon visit, however, especially from May to the first half of June, when 100,000 brightly colored tulips burst into bloom.

Finally, when you're ready for thrills (hopefully, no spills), hop on the old wooden roller coaster. Built in 1914, its incessant creaking gives riders a real reason to scream. If you need a drink to steady your nerves afterward, head for **Groften** or **Slukefter.** The former, parts of which are open year round, serves Danish food, and the latter, located beside the main entrance to Tivoli, features jazz and blues year round.

The **Tivolis Billetcenter (Tivoli Ticket Center),** Vesterbrogade 3 (tel. 33/15-10-12), sells tickets to concerts and special events in the park. This office also distributes a free daily schedule, and is located next to the park's main entrance.

Admission: 28 Kr ($4.90) for adults, 14 Kr ($2.45) if you arrive

Alexander Nevsky Church 7
Amaliehavn Gardens 10
Amalienborg Palace 9
Benneweis Circus 33
Borsen 25
Botansk Have 14
Botansk Museum 13
Charlottenborg Palace 24
Christiansborg Palace 27
Frihedsmuseet 4
Geologisk Museet 15
Helligåndskirke 22
Hirschsprung Collection 17
Kastellet 2
Kongelige Bibliotek 28
Kongelige Teater 23
Kunstindustrimuseet 5
Legetøjsmuseet 20
Little Mermaid 1
Louis Tussaud's Wax Museum 35
Marble Church 8
Museum of Applied Art 34
National Museet 31
Ny Carlsberg Glyptotek 37
Observatory 11
Rådhus 32
Rosenborg Castle 12
Runde Tårn 18
St. Albans 3
St. Ansgar's 6
Scala Center 38
Statens Museum for Kunst 16
Teater Historisk Museet 30
Thorvaldsen Museet 26
Tivoli 36
Tøjhusmuseet 29
University 19

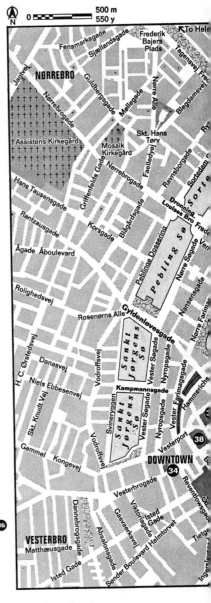

before 1pm; half price for children under 12. Rides cost 10–15 Kr ($1.75–$2.65) each; an unlimited-ride ticket is available.

Open: Park, daily 10am–midnight; Ticket Center, Mon–Sat noon–6pm (also on Sun when events are scheduled). **Closed:** Third week of Sept to the third week in Apr. **Directions:** Walk from the city center.

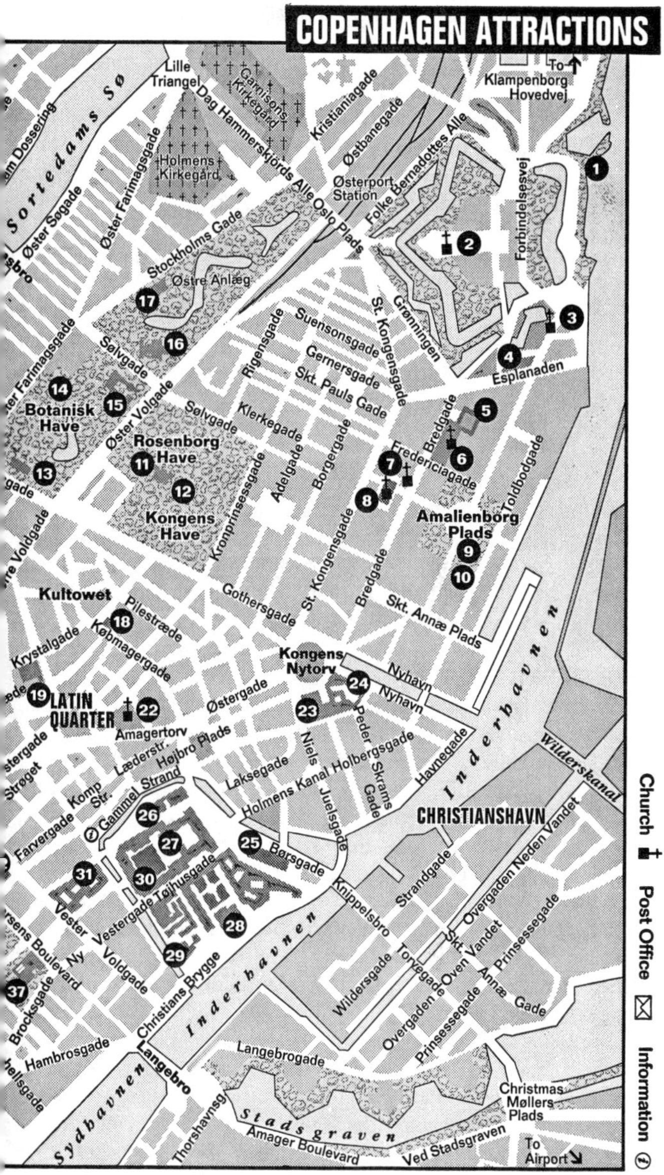

COPENHAGEN ATTRACTIONS

ROSENBORG CASTLE, Øster Voldgade 4a. Tel. 33/15-32-86.

The summer residence of King Christian IV (1577–1648) was built during his reign and served as the official royal residence throughout the 17th century. Today, some of the castle's most interesting parts are open to the public: the opulently furnished State

Apartments and a dungeon containing the kingdom's most valued jewels and possessions. The valuables, guarded by armed troops and steel doors, include jewel-encrusted swords, dazzling crowns, opulent necklaces, and other priceless possessions of the royal family, some of which are still worn by the queen at state functions. When the queen is in residence at Amalienborg Palace, the Royal Guard leaves Rosenborg Palace daily at 11:30am and marches there for a Changing of the Guard ceremony; the old guard then marches back from Amalienborg to Rosenborg.

The well-preserved upstairs rooms and the sculpted gardens are equally wondrous. The diminutive size of the redbrick, Dutch Renaissance–style castle makes it far less daunting (and time-consuming to explore) than most other Danish castles. Christian IV came back here to die in 1648. The palace has been open to the public since 1833.

Admission: 35 Kr ($6.15) for adults, 17 Kr ($3) for students, 7 Kr ($1.20) for children under 15. Prices are about 30% lower in winter.

Open: May–Aug daily 10am–3pm; Sept–Oct daily 11am–3pm; the rest of the year, Tues–Sun 11am–3pm (the imperial jewels are open to view only Tues, Fri, and Sun 11am–2pm). **S-tog:** Nørreport. **Bus:** No. 5, 7, 10, 14, 16, 43, 73E, or 84.

AMALIENBORG PALACE, Slotsplads.

The official residence of Denmark's Queen Margrethe (Margaret) II and her husband, Prince Henrik, is an outstanding example of rococo architecture. Amalienborg is actually a complex of four palaces dating from 1760 that ring around a large cobblestone square. An equestrian statue of Frederik V stands at the center of the square, while the Queen's Guards—bearskin hats and all—stand watch around the perimeter. The noontime Changing of the Guard at Amalienborg is as spirited as any, full of pomp and pageantry. The ritual, performed only when the queen is in residence (mainly during the colder months), begins with an 11:30am assembly at Rosenborg Palace. The soldiers then march to Amalienborg Palace for the Changing of the Guard.

The palace interiors are not open to the public, but Amalienborg (and the surrounding community) is truly worth a visit—even when guard-changing ceremonies are not scheduled.

As you enter the square (the Marble Church, the large domed church, should be directly in front of you), the queen's residence is immediately to your left; the queen's mother lives in the mansion to your right; beyond it, also on the right, is the residence of the queen's sons, crown princes Frederik and Joachim, who are in their early twenties (quite a bachelor pad, isn't it?). The mansion opposite it, to your left, is used only for court functions. If flags are flying out front, the royal residents are at home. If you arrive on April 16, the queen's birthday, expect to see her waving from the balcony during an extra-special Changing of the Guard ceremony.

Amalienborg has been the royal residence since 1794.

(Amalienhavns Kiosk, a block from the palace, at Toldbødgade 34, where the tour buses stop, sells cards, souvenirs, stamps, sandwiches, and ice cream, and has a telephone and rest room; friendly owner Poul Jensen is a wealth of information.)

RUNDETÅRN (The Round Tower), Købmagergade. Tel. 33/93-66-60.

There are taller buildings in the city, boasting more spectacular views, but none has more charm and history than this ancient observatory. Built by King Christian IV in 1642, the Round Tower has long been loved by locals as an integral part of the cityscape. The observation platform up top can only be reached by climbing the tower's internal spiral ramp. On the way up, you'll pass a large gallery with changing exhibits; it's free and worth a look. At the observation platform, maps point out prominent rooftops around the old city, Rosenborg Castle in the foreground, and Frederiksberg Castle on the horizon.

Admission: 10 Kr ($1.75) for adults, 4 Kr (70¢) for children.

Open: Mon–Sat 10am–5pm, Sun noon–4pm; during the winter, the observatory is open Tues–Wed 7–10pm.

Directions: Walk from the city center.

DEN LILLE HAVFRUE (Little Mermaid), Langelinie on the harbor.

Like famous monuments the world over, this simple green statue on a rock off the shore will seem smaller than you had imagined it, but it will make you smile all the same. Locals poke fun at the statue's popularity, and at times have even vandalized it. Still, this frail bronze figure, created in 1913 by Edvard Eriksen and inspired by the Hans Christian Andersen fairy tale, remains the most famous monument in Copenhagen.

The model for the statue was a ballerina with the Royal Ballet. It was given to the city in 1913 by brewery magnate Carl Jacobsen, 76 years after the beloved fairy tale was published. Late one night in 1964, the mermaid's head was sawed off, never to be seen again, but another was made immediately from the original cast. This is actually the second mermaid statue Eriksen made for the harbor; the first, exactly like it but even more diminutive, was rejected by Jacobsen as too small and now sits on the Carlsberg Brewery grounds.

The long stretch of quay beyond the sculpture, called Langelinie, harbors visiting cruise and naval vessels. The unfortunate background for the Little Mermaid (particularly for photographers) is the unsightly Brumeister and Wain Shipyard.

Adjacent to the statue, **Kastellet Park,** laid out on the remains of Copenhagen's old ramparts, is a beautiful area for strolling and picnicking. Don't miss Gefion Fountain or the bust of Winston Churchill, adjacent to St. Alban's Church.

Bus: No. 1, 6, or 9; during the summer a shuttle bus operates between Town Hall Square and the statue. **S-tog:** Østerport; then walk through the park.

CHRISTIANSBORG PALACE, Christiansborg Slotsplads, on Slotsholmen. Tel. 33/92-64-92.

Rebuilt early in this century on top of 800-year-old foundations, Christiansborg Palace was home to the Swedish royal family until 1794. The ring of water surrounding the tiny island of Slotsholmen resembles a protective moat. Most of the palace's rooms are now used as offices by parliamentary and supreme court officials, though a few of the glamorous royal reception rooms still serve their original purpose. On the second and fourth Monday of each month, Danish "commoners" can request an audience with the queen here. For tourists, admission is by guided tour only, and features the Throne Room, where the queen receives foreign ambassadors; the Velvet Room, named for its hanging tapestries; and the Banquet Hall, still used by the royal family and their guests of honor. These and other rooms are resplendent with Murano chandeliers, Flemish tapestries, and other impressive details. The palace entrance is beyond the large courtyard, on the left side of the building.

For additional charges, you may also visit the palace ruins (the original foundations of Bishop Absalon's 1167 castle), the royal stables, and the palace theater, where Hans Christian Andersen performed at age 14.

Admission: 20 Kr ($3.50) for adults, 10 Kr ($1.75) for children.

Open: Tours given May–Sept, Tues–Sun at 11am, 1pm, and 3pm; Oct–Apr and Jan, Tues–Fri and Sun at 11am and 1pm. **Closed:** Mid-Dec to Jan. **Bus:** No. 1, 2, 5, 8, 9, 10, 31, 37, or 43.

NY CARLSBERG GLYPTOTEK, Dantes Plads, at the southeast corner of Tivoli. Tel. 33/91-10-65.

Specializing in ancient art, the Glyptotek has amassed impressive collections of Roman statues, Egyptian sarcophagi, Greek reliefs, and other Mediterranean objects. Founded by brewer/arts patron Carl Jacobsen in 1882, the collection of antiquities has continued to grow, along with extensive works from more recent times. The second-floor modernists are mainly French and include Gauguin, Picasso, van Gogh, Monet, Cézanne, Renoir, and Degas (don't miss Gallery 28).

The museum is built around a huge botanical courtyard with "The Water Mother" by Kai Nelson at its center. Both peaceful and quiet, it's not unusual for locals to visit the Glyptotek without any intention of looking at art.

Admission: 15 Kr ($2.65); free Wed and Sun, and at all times for children.

Open: May–Aug, daily 10am–4pm; rest of year, Tues–Sat noon–3pm, Sun 10am–4pm. **Closed:** Christmas, Good Friday, Easter, Whitsunday, June 5. **S-tog:** Hovedbanegård.

STATENS MUSEUM FOR KUNST (State Museum of Fine Art), Sølvgade 48-50. Tel. 33/91-21-26.

The country's largest art museum occupies a monumental building in the Østre Anlæg park. The Danish art is separated from all the rest, and although there is heavy emphasis on works from the late 18th century, most are overshadowed by outstanding 19th-century landscapes. The foreign art section is heavy on Dutch and Flemish paintings, though other European modernists (especially French), such as Matisse and Braque, are also well represented. Look for special changing exhibitions.

If you collect museum postcards, this is a great place to come.

Admission: Free.

Open: Tues–Sun 10am–4:30pm. **Bus:** No. 10 or 184.

OUTSIDE THE CITY

LOUISIANA MUSEUM OF MODERN ART, Gammel Strandvej 13, Humlebæk. Tel. 42/19-07-19.

Located in North Zealand 30km (18.6 miles) from Copenhagen, and definitely worth the half-hour train ride to get there, this modern art repository is Denmark's most visited museum. It takes its name from the wives (all three of them) of the original owner of the estate, a noted horticulturist and beekeeper named Alexander Brun. The museum was founded in 1958 by Knud Jensen, a cheese tycoon.

The permanent collection includes several works by Warhol, Lichtenstein, Calder, and Giacometti. Admittedly, the world-class special exhibitions are usually the main draw, spotlighting the works of Chagall, Dali, and Warhol, for instance. But the museum, itself, on a spectacular parcel of land overlooking the ocean, is a beautiful place to visit no matter what's on. During warmer months you can picnic on the grounds.

Admission: Special round-trip rail ticket of 64 Kr ($11.20) includes museum entrance. Free for Copenhagen Card holders; otherwise, 40 Kr ($7) for adults, free for children.

Open: Mon–Tues and Thurs–Sun, 10am–5pm; Wed 10am–10pm. **Directions:** Take a train (departures 3 times an hour) from

Central Station platform 1 or 2 to Humlebæk station, then walk the scenic mile to the museum or take bus no. 388. Follow the signs (and the crowds).

2. MORE ATTRACTIONS

CHRISTIANA, Christianshavn.

Organized squatters took over dozens of disused army buildings on the island of Christianshavn in 1971, creating the "Free State of Christiania." The public, both critical of the city's housing situation and curious about this new solution, generally supported the group, pressuring the government against taking any action. Today, Christianians, some 900 of them, support their own government, paying taxes and rent to Christiania instead of the Danish government. "Why should I go outside Christiania?" one resident asked. "It satisfies my every need." In reality, however, many residents do accept the benefits of Denmark's social welfare system and leave Christiania for medical and other needs.

The area, with its piles of garbage, dirt, graffiti, unpaved streets, and sometimes open drug use, looks more like an undeveloped nation than modern Denmark. But these unsightly things are offset by interesting murals, wonderfully painted houses, and even a gallery and some nightspots. Tourists are welcome, but they are asked not to take photographs, especially along the main drag, known as "Pusher Street." A popular restaurant and jazz club, **Spiseloppen** and **Loppen,** are located in the building to your right just inside the main entrance to Christiania; rest rooms and a small gallery are in the same building.

Bus: No. 8 from Town Hall Square; get off at the second stop after Knippels Bridge.

FRIHEDSMUSEET (Denmark's Fight for Freedom Museum 1940–45), Churchillparken. Tel. 33/13-77-14.

This small but fascinating collection chronicles the nation's underground fight against the Germans who, despite Denmark's pledge of neutrality, occupied the country in 1940. Computerized information, an audiovisual presentation, and exhibits on sabotage efforts and prison life, along with a plethora of pictures, are featured. The museum also celebrates the nation's unique efforts to save the country's Jewish citizens. Be sure to pick up the free 40-page guide upon entering.

Admission: Free.

Open: May to mid-Sept, Tues–Sat 10am–4pm, Sun 10am–5pm;

FROMMER'S FAVORITE COPENHAGEN EXPERIENCES

A stroll along Strøget The ambience, shops, street entertainers, and sheer length of the street make it an experience found nowhere else in the world.

Tea and pastries at La Glace Do as the Danes have done since 1870. The pastries, and the café itself, are out of this world.

An evening at Tivoli Aglow with more than 110,000 lights, it mixes exotic architecture, world-class entertainment, and lively cafés to create its own infectious magic.

A day at Louisiana One of the world's finest modern art museums, and surely the most dramatically situated, it's a jewel on the Øresund.

A foray into North Zealand Experience the delightful Danish countryside via the Strandvejen, or Coast Road, stopping along the way to visit Rungstedlund, home of author Isak Dinesen; the Louisiana Museum of Modern Art; and windswept Kronborg Castle, Hamlet's fictional home.

rest of year, Tues–Sat 11am–3pm, Sun 11am–4pm. **S-tog:** Østerport.

NATIONAL MUSEUM, Frederiksholms Kanal 12. Tel. 33/13-44-11.

Cataloging life in Denmark since the Stone Age, this vast museum, located across from Christiansborg Castle, includes prehistoric finds, ancient burial chambers, traditional farmers' tools, and centuries-old porcelain, furniture, and housewares. Interesting, too, are the displays on the colonization of Greenland. The museum keeps very limited hours, and even though it's often jammed with schoolchildren during the week, it's still worth a visit. There are guided tours in English.

Admission: Free, except the Victorian House, which is 12 Kr ($2.10) for adults, 5 Kr (90¢) for children.

Open: June 16–Sept 15, Tues–Sun 10am–4pm; rest of year, Tues–Fri 11am–3pm and Sat–Sun noon–4pm. Victorian House has restricted hours. **Bus:** No. 1, 2, 5, 6, or 10.

KØBENHAVNS RÅDHUS (Town Hall), Rådhuspladsen. Tel. 33/15-38-00.

Copenhagen's imposing red-brick Town Hall (1905) is one of the best-known structures in the city and is most famous for **Jens Olsen's World Clock,** a giant silver-and-gold timepiece located on the ground floor. Since it began ticking in 1955, the clock has faithfully kept track of local time, solar time, sunrise and sunset times, the migration of the celestial pole, and the Gregorian and Julian calendars—and is accurate to within half a second every 300 years!

Admission: Town Hall 10 Kr ($1.75) for adults and children; clock 8Kr ($1.40) for adults, 5 Kr (90¢) for children.

Open: Guided tours, Mon–Fri at 1pm and Sat at 10am; Jens Olsen's World Clock, Mon–Sat 10am–3pm.

MUSEUM OF DECORATIVE AND APPLIED ART (Kunstindustrimuseet), Bredgade 68. Tel. 33/14-94-52.

Housed in a former hospital, the stately museum is laid out around a large garden. Its special exhibits never fail to create excitement; the permanent collection is ho-hum by comparison. A small café is on the premises. Note the limited hours.

Admission: Free Tues–Fri Sept–June; weekends year round and Tues–Fri in July–Aug, 20 Kr ($3.50) for adults; free for children.

Open: Tues–Sun 1–4pm.

THE WORKERS' MUSEUM (Arbejdermuseet), Rømersgade 22. Tel. 33/13-01-52.

Rarely does a museum portray the life of common folk. This one does, in three permanent exhibits: "For Life and Bread," about the effect of industrialization on Danish lives in 1870; "Meager Times," about unemployment in the 1930s; and "The 1950s," depicting the prosperous times following World War II. The museum's restaurant, Café & Ol-Halle 1892, looks like cafés did 100 years ago, and it serves food and drink from that era, as well.

Admission: 20 Kr ($3.50) for adults, 10 Kr ($1.75) for seniors and children.

Open: Mon–Tues and Thurs–Sun 11am–4pm; Wed 11am–8pm. **S-tog:** Nørreport.

CHURCHES

This city of spires and steeples has many churches of note, and you only have to be in Copenhagen a short time before they make their ages-old presence felt. Most are open to the public during the day.

IN THE CENTER

THE MARBLE CHURCH (Marmokirken), just off Amalienborg Palace square, Frederiksgade. Tel. 33/15-37-63.

A striking part of Amalienborg Square, the massive domed church got its name from the Norwegian marble from which it is made. The dome is the largest dome in Scandinavia. The church—which was consecrated in 1894, 145 years after its foundation was laid—lines up with the equestrian statue of King Frederik V at Amalienborg Palace Square and the fountain at Amalienhavn.

ST. NICHOLAS CHURCH (Sankt Nicolaj Kirke), just off Strøget at Amagertorv.

A familiar sight to pedestrians milling about Strøget, the church dates only from 1914, but its steeple has stood on this spot since the Middle Ages. The building is no longer used for religious services but for special exhibitions sponsored by the Borough of Copenhagen.

RUSSIAN ORTHODOX CHURCH (St. Alexander Nevsky), Bredgade 53. Tel. 33/13-60-46.

With its unmistakable onion domes, it looks like an escapee from *Dr. Zhivago* and is a lovely but surprising sight on Bredgade.

ST. ALBANS CHURCH, in Churchill Park, Langelinie. Tel. 31/62-77-36.

Also known as the English Church (it's Anglican Episcopalian), it sits simply and peacefully (looking much like a country church) in Churchill Park. Gefion Fountain, behind it, is much splashier. The church is a short walk from the Little Mermaid.

VOR FRUE KIRKE (Our Lady's Church or The Cathedral), Nørregade. Tel. 33/14-41-28.

In the heart of the university area, it lacks the architectural majesty of most cathedrals; for that, you'll have to visit Roskilde (see "Easy Excursions from Copenhagen," Chapter 10).

IN CHRISTIANSHAVN

CHURCH OF OUR SAVIOR (Vor Freslsers Kirke), Sankt Annægade at Prinsessegade. Tel. 31/57-27-98.

Built in 1682, this baroque church has a most unusual spiral tower with an outdoor 400-step staircase, which you can climb for a glorious view. At the top is a gilt statue of Christ standing on a globe.

CHRISTIAN'S CHURCH (Christians Kirke), Strandgade. Tel. 31/54-15-76.

This church (built from 1755 to 1759) is rococo in style except for its classical steeple. Its interior is designed like a theater with boxes in three tiers.

OUTSIDE THE CITY

GRUNDTVIGS KIRKE (Grundtvig's Church), På Bjerget. Tel. 31/81-54-42.

This impressive blonde-brick structure—a cross between a simple Danish church (no stained glass, no grand altar) and a Gothic cathedral—was built to honor N. F. S. Grundtvig, the Lutheran parson, poet, and founder of the folk high school movement. The model ship hanging inside was a gift from Queen Alexandrine (Queen Margrethe's grandmother). The church (completed in 1940) measures 22 meters (70 ft.) high on the inside, with a tower soaring 35 meters (111 ft.). Each of its massive columns is made of 10,000 to 12,000 bricks. Concerts are held here in summer.

Admission: Free.

Open: Mid-May to mid-Sept, Mon–Sat 9am–4:45pm, Sun noon–4pm; mid-Sept to mid-May Mon–Sat 9am–4pm, Sun noon–1pm, except when there is an official church function. **Bus:** No. 19 from Town Hall.

PARKS & GARDENS

In addition to the gardens of **Tivoli,** Copenhagen boasts several other greens that are perfect for picnicking.

On the grounds of Rosenborg Palace the sculptured gardens of **Kongens Have** attract ducks, swans, gulls, and people. This is the city's oldest park, and is as popular as ever with hand-holders and strollers alike.

The charming, wooded **Botanisk Have (Botanical Garden),** behind the State Museum of Fine Art, is particularly nice on hot summer days. The gates are open daily from 8:30am to 6pm, April to October; until 4pm the rest of the year.

Like most parks in the city, the **Park of the Citadel (Kastellet),** behind the *Little Mermaid,* is laid out on Copenhagen's old ramparts. Adjacent **Churchill Park,** to the south, is noted for St. Alban's English Church and the impressive Gefion Fountain, depicting the legend of the founding of Denmark.

A ribbon of three artificial lakes cuts through Copenhagen (all rectangular and uninspiring); the most appealing, **Lake Peblinge,** is the scene of enthusiastic boating, strolling, sitting, and duck feeding in summer. Nearby, **Ørsteds Park,** with its small lake, pleasant paths, and statues, invites meandering. Cemetery lovers won't be disappointed by the parklike **Assistens Kirkegard,** at Nørrebrogade and Kapelvej, the final resting place of Hans Christian Andersen, Søren Kierkegaard, physicists H. C. Orsted and Niels Bohr, and tenor sax player Ben Webster.

North of the city center on Tuborgvej is **Mindelunden i Ryvangen** (The Memorial Park), dedicated to Danish civilians who lost their lives during the Nazi occupation—from April 9, 1940 to May 5, 1945. Buried here are those 31 Danish Jews who died in concentration camps. The location of the park is a former Nazi execution site. To visit, take the S-tog to Ryparken.

In Frederiksberg, west of the city center, are two lovely parks. Both are within walking distance of the Carlsberg Brewery and may easily be combined with a visit there. The **Sondermarken** is more forest than park and a favorite spot of locals for ambling and dog walking. **Frederiksberg Have,** adjacent to the zoo and one of the city's prettiest parks, features an 18th-century palace that now houses a military academy. **Fælledparken,** a popular spot for outdoor concerts in summer, has existed since 1910.

PLAZAS & PUBLIC SQUARES

Copenhagen is particularly well blessed with open squares. Mile-long Strøget is bookended by two of them: **Town Hall Square** and **Kongens Nytorv,** where you'll find the Royal Theater and Hotel d'Angleterre, grand dame of Copenhagen hotels.

As you meander Strøget, you'll pass three other squares: **Gammel Torv (Old Square),** Copenhagen's oldest market square, dating from the 15th century, with Caritas Fountain as its centerpiece; **Ny Torv (New Square),** opposite Gammel Torv and a couple of centuries its junior; and **Amagertorv,** with the whimsical Stork Fountain.

Højbro Plads, just south of Amagertorv at Gammel Strand, is best known for the equestrian statue of Bishop Absalon; Absalon is said to have tethered his horse at this spot when he founded the city.

Gråbrødre Torv (Greyfriars Square), in the very center of the city and as old as Copenhagen itself, is a popular gathering spot for locals, who lounge under the large plane tree at its center or at a nearby outdoor café. In the summer, the square blossoms with street entertainers and occasional live music concerts. It's a couple of blocks north of Strøget via Neils Hemmingsens Gade.

Kultorvet (Coal Square), a center of activity for university students, is north of Gråbrødre Torv, at Købmagergade and Rosengården.

Israels Plads, nestled between the Botanical Garden and Ørsteds Park, used to be the city's main vegetable market; fruits, vegetables, and flowers are still sold here, except on Saturday when it becomes a large flea market.

Amalienhavn, the plaza between Amalienborg Palace and the harbor, was donated in 1983 by A. P. Moller, owner of Mærsk Line. A giant fountain is its focal point. The limestone and granite in the plaza come from Denmark's only rocky island, Bornholm.

3. COOL FOR KIDS

TIVOLI *(see page 93)* The little ones love the Pantomime Theater, where Pierrot, Columbine, and Harlequin perform Monday through Saturday nights. Teens love the thrilling ride of the wooden roller coaster that's been a fixture since 1914. The grounds of Tivoli are visual magic to kids of all ages, day or night.

LOUIS TUSSAUD'S WAX MUSEUM, H. C. Andersens Blvd. 22. Tel. 33/14-29-22.

Sound effects add to the wonder of scenes from the Brothers Grimm, Sleeping Beauty, Jack and the Bean Stalk, and the Snow Queen. For the very brave, there's a spooky Chamber of Horrors.

Admission: 17 Kr ($3) for kids, 40 Kr ($7) for adults.

Open: Late Apr to mid-Sept, daily 10am–11pm; mid-Sept to late Apr, daily 10am–4:30pm. **S-tog:** Hovedbanegård.

TYCHO BRAHE PLANETARIUM, Gammel Kongevej 10. Tel. 33/12-12-24.

Western Europe's largest planetarium, it opened in 1990 and looks like a can with the top sliced off at an angle. Named after the 16th-century Danish astronomer who built the world's first modern observatory and proved that stars are not fixed objects—it has a state-of-the-art star projector, permanent and special exhibits, an Omnimax theater, and conveniently long hours.

Admission: To exhibits 10 Kr ($1.75); for Omnimax movies, add another 45–85 Kr ($7.90–$14.90), depending on the show.

Open: Mon–Sun 10:30am–9pm, Tues–Thurs 8:30am–9pm, Fri–Sat 10:30am–10pm. **S-tog:** Vesterport. **Bus:** No. 6, 7, 28, or 41.

IMPRESSIONS

Really, I should drop these trifles [fairy tales] and concentrate on my own work.

—HANS CHRISTIAN ANDERSEN

EKSPERIMENTARIUM (Science Hall), Tuborg Brewery, Strandvejen 54. Tel. 39/27-33-33.

Newly opened in 1991 and housed in the old bottling hall at Tuborg Brewery, it takes a hands-on approach to popular technology and the natural sciences.

Admission: 30–50 Kr ($5.25–$8.80).

Open: Mon, Wed, and Fri–Sun 9am–6pm; Tues and Thurs 9am–9pm. **S-tog:** Hellerup. **Bus:** No. 6.

LEGETOJSMUSEET (The Toy Museum), Valkendorfsgade 13. Tel. 33/14-10-09.

It houses almost 5,000 toys from Denmark, Germany, England, and the United States in a converted, 200-year-old warehouse. The first floor is a re-created Danish village, with 14 houses, each displaying toys with a different theme. Dolls and dollhouses fill the top floor. The oldest toy dates from 1540, and the 1740 Noah's Ark still has all its animals. One exhibit, "Doll Doctor," is a 1920's doll shop stocked with spare body parts.

Admission: 10 Kr ($1.75) for kids, 20 Kr ($3.50) for grownups.

Open: Mon–Thurs 9am–4pm, Sat–Sun 10am–4pm. **S-tog:** Nørreport.

ZOOLOGISK HAVE (Copenhagen Zoo), Roskildevej 32. Tel. 36/30-20-01.

Founded in 1859 and modernized in recent years, it is home to more than 2,500 animals, from Nordic species to Asiatic black bears and South American llamas. Open year-round, there is a special activity-playground area for children.

Admission: 20 Kr ($3.50) for kids, 40 Kr ($7) for adults.

Open: Daily 9am–6pm. **Bus:** No. 28, 29, or 41 to the door.

BENNEWEIS CIRCUS, Circus Building, Axeltorv at Vesterbrogade. Tel. 33/14-44-32 (box office 33/14-21-92).

In the heart of Copenhagen in a confection of a building, the Benneweis Circus has been thrilling Danish children for four generations, combining magic, comedy, dance, lasers, and all the circus attractions kids love so well.

Admission: 40–110 Kr ($7–$19.30).

Open: Box office, day of performance, 1–8pm. Performances, mid-May to late Oct, Tues–Fri, 8pm; Thurs 4pm and 8pm; Sun 4pm. **S-tog:** Hovedbanegård.

OUTSIDE THE CITY

BAKKEN, Klampenborg. Tel. 31/63-73-00.

Its name means "The Hill," and at 400 and counting, it's the oldest amusement park in the world and only 10km (6 miles) from Copenhagen. There are 120 attractions, rides, and eateries, as well as two daily performances on an open-air stage. Kids love Pierrot who swallows fire and performs in the Punch and Judy shows. If you're staying at the beach, it's just a pebble's throw away (check "Accommodations—North of the Center Near the Beach," in Chapter 4).

Admission: Free.

Open: End of Mar–end of Aug, daily noon–midnight. **S-tog:** Klampenborg; it's a five-minute walk or quick horse-drawn carriage ride from here along Dyrehavevej. **Bus:** No. 27, 160, or 176 to Klampenborg.

OPEN-AIR MUSEUM (FRILANDSMUSEET), Kongevejen 100, Lyngby. Tel. 42/85-02-92.

You'll see many old farms, windmills, and houses that have been brought here from all over Denmark and assembled in 40 tranquil acres.

Admission: 15 Kr ($2.65) for adults, 5 Kr (90¢) for children.

Open: Mid-Mar to Sept, Tues–Sun 10am–5pm; Oct to mid-Nov, Tues–Sun 10am–3pm. **Closed:** Mid-Nov to mid-Mar. **S-tog:** Sorgenfri. **Bus:** No. 184.

PILGRIMAGES FOR KIDS

LEGOLAND, Billund. Tel. 75/33-13-33.

Kids who treasure their own cache of Lego bricks are struck dumb by the sheer magnitude of Legoland, with more than 33 million bricks. Favorite attractions in this unique Danish family park include the Wild West town of Legoredo, a model of Mount Rushmore with 1.5 million bricks, and a miniature palace made of 3,000 bricks—the stuff children's dreams are made of. One- and two-day tours from Copenhagen to Legoland are available June through mid-September; ask about them at the tourist office.

Admission: 22 Kr ($3.85) for kids; 44 Kr ($7.70) for adults.

Open: Late Apr to mid-Sept. **Directions:** Train to Billund.

HANS CHRISTIAN ANDERSEN'S MUSEUM (H. C. Andersen Hus), 39 Hans Jensensstræde, Odense, Funen. Tel. 66/13-13-72.

Hans Christian Andersen grew up in Odense, on the island of Funen, so it's fitting that the memorabilia of his life are collected here. You'll see everything from his signature top hat to his famous walking stick, along with his correspondence to Charles Dickens and Jenny Lind, manuscripts, and copies of his books of fairy tales in many languages. The museum is open in April, May, and September from 10am to 5pm; June through August from 9am to 6pm; and October through March 10am to 3pm.

Andersen's birthplace, **H. C. Andersens Barndomshjem** (same telephone as above), a small cottage with a garden, is also in Odense. The author lived here from age 2 to 14, when he left school and his home and set off for Copenhagen to seek his fortune. (He ultimately found it, but he finished school first!) Andersen's childhood was one he was probably happy to leave behind him, but he supposedly loved the cottage, which is open to the public from April through September from 10am to 5pm, and October through March from noon to 3pm.

Tours from Copenhagen to Odense are offered from mid-May to mid-September; check at the tourist office.

4. SPECIAL-INTEREST SIGHTSEEING

FOR HISTORY BUFFS

TØJHUSMUSEET (Royal Arsenal Museum), Tøjhusgade 3. Tel. 31/11-60-37.

Those who believe the history of humanity is the history of war will find much of interest here. Housed in the king's arsenal, completed in 1604 with the longest arched hall in Europe, this museum displays a vast collection of weapons spanning several

IMPRESSIONS

The community of the people is shaped by history; a people can only maintain its identity and protect its responsibility to the future if it lives with its past.

—J. C. JACOBSEN, BENEFACTOR, AND FOUNDER OF CARLSBERG BREWERY

centuries. The first floor, a veritable forest of steel, features tank and artillery displays as well as a long series of cannons. Several airplanes, including two 1927 craft and a 1911 propeller plane, hang from the ceiling. The thousands of personal weapons on the second floor include armor pieces, guns, and swords.

Admission: Free.

Open: May–Sept, Tues–Sat 1–4pm and Sun 10am–4pm; rest of year, Tues–Sat 1–3pm and Sun 11am–4pm.

FREDERIKSBORG PALACE, Hillerød. Tel. 42/26-04-39.

This incomparable palace, a not-so-scenic, 45-minute ride from Copenhagen, has been called the "Versailles of Northern Europe." It was built in Dutch Renaissance style as a royal residence from 1600 to 1621 for Christian IV, who was king of Denmark and Norway for 60 years. Of particular interest are the immense Neptune Fountain, the elaborate, restored three-dimensional ceiling in the Knights Hall, and the chapel, looking just as it did when Christian IV used it.

Admission: 25 Kr ($4.40) for adults, 10 Kr ($1.75) for students, and 5 Kr (90¢) for children 6 to 14. Tour cassettes are available in English for 20 Kr ($3.50).

Open: Apr and Oct, daily 10am–4pm; May–Sept, daily 10am–5pm; Nov–Mar, daily 11am–3pm. **Directions:** Take a bus or train to Hillerød or link up with a tour from Copenhagen.

FREDENSBORG PALACE, Fredensborg. Tel. 42/28-18-35.

This official royal residence (spring and fall) is closed to the public year round except for the month of July. Called the "Castle of Peace," it was built (1719–22) by Frederik IV to commemorate the end of war with Sweden. Be sure to stroll the grounds (open year round) on which this Danish-Italian–style palace sits overlooking Lake Esrum, Denmark's second largest lake. You might even see Queen Margrethe and Prince Henrik strolling in the gardens.

Admission: 7.50 Kr ($1.30) for adults, 3 Kr (50¢) for children.

Open: July only, daily 1–5pm. **Train:** Fredensborg. **Bus:** No. 336 or 384.

FOR ART & ARCHITECTURE BUFFS

THORVALDSEN MUSEUM, Slotsholmen. Tel. 33/32-15-32.

The personal museum of Bertel Thorvaldsen (1770–1844), Denmark's most celebrated sculptor, features the artist's graceful creations as well as other works from his private collection. Most notable are Thorvaldsen's plaster casts of large monuments from around the world. The museum is adjacent to Christiansborg Palace.

Admission: Free.

Open: Tues–Sun 10am–5pm. **Directions:** Walk from the town center.

KØBENHAVNS BYMUSEUM (Copenhagen City Museum), Vesterbrogade 59. Tel. 31/21-07-72.

Many pictures, prints, maps, and models of Copenhagen illustrate the development of the city from antiquity to the present day. A separate, permanent display features objects associated with the life of philosopher and author Søren Kierkegaard.

Admission: Free.

Open: May–Sept, Tues–Sun 10am–4pm; rest of year, Tues–Sun 1–4pm. **Bus:** No. 6, 16, 28, or 41.

DANSK ARKITEKTURCENTER, Strandgade 27b. Tel. 31/57-19-30.

Changing exhibitions emphasize modern developments in Danish architecture.

Admission: 20 Kr ($3.50) for adults, free for children.

Open: Tues–Sun 10am–5pm (until 10pm Wed). **Bus:** No. 2, 8, 9, 31, or 37.

DAVIDS SAMLING (The David Collection), Kronprinsessegade 30. Tel. 33/13-62-13.

The former home of lawyer, businessman, and art collector C. L. David, who died in 1962, it purportedly houses the largest collection of Islamic art outside the Islamic countries. Beautiful calligraphy, pottery, tiles, and tapestries are on the fourth floor; the first three floors are devoted to Danish, French, and English art and decorative arts, respectively.

Admission: Free.

Open: Tues–Sun 1–4pm. **Directions:** Across the street from Rosenborg Park.

5. ORGANIZED TOURS

WALKING TOURS

The Guide Ring, Kongelundsvej 91 (tel. 31/51-25-90), under the direction of Mr. H. S. Jacobsen, offers a diverse selection of English-language walking tours during summer months only. Walks begin at different sites and times depending on subject, so call ahead for complete information. Prices are usually 25 Kr ($4.40) for adults,

20 Kr ($3.50) for students to 23 years old, free for children. Walks are also listed in the tourist board publication *Copenhagen This Week*.

"Copenhagen on Foot," an excellent brochure distributed free by Use-It (see "Tourist Information," Chapter 3, for address), will guide you through the streets of the city at your own pace. (See also Chapter 7, "Strolling Around Copenhagen.")

BUS TOURS

Use-It's free **"Copenhagen by Bus"** brochure takes you through a do-it-yourself tour of all the major sights using city bus no. 6. Those looking for more structure can choose from over a dozen guided bus tours. **Vikingbus** (tel. 31/57-26-00) offers a 2½-hour "Grand Tour of Copenhagen" at 150 Kr ($24.55) for adults, half price for children under 12. Tours depart from Town Hall Square April through October daily at 11am and 1:30pm (also at 3pm from mid-September to mid-October); the rest of the year, daily at 11am (also on Saturday at 1:30pm).

BOAT TOURS

Though no longer as active as it was years ago, the city's waterfront has remained as impressive and interesting as ever. Complemented by a vast network of canals running through the old part of the city, boat tours offer both a relaxing cruise and a good education on the history of the city. Guided tours run from May to the middle of September only, cost 35 Kr ($6.15) for adults and 15 Kr ($2.65) for children, last about 1 hour, and depart every 30 minutes from both Gammel Strand and Kongens Nytorv.

There is also a half-hour unguided tour to the Little Mermaid for 24 Kr ($4.20); another, called "Under 12 Bridges," explores the city's canals for 28 Kr ($4.90); kids pay half price for either. Check with the tourist board for times and itineraries for all tours.

BREWERY TOURS

CARLSBERG BREWERY, Valby Langgade 1. Tel. 31/21-12-21, ext. 1312.

This guided tour shows how barley, hops, yeast, and water are combined to make the famous Carlsberg beer. The main brewing hall dates from the turn of the century and is dominated by huge copper kettles and a pungent aroma. The bottling hall is the tour's highlight, filling and capping more than 78,000 bottles an hour! The hour-long tour concludes with a visit to the beer museum, and free samples of the brewery's products.

Additional highlights are the unique Elephant Gate and the original Little(r) Mermaid. A visit here may easily be combined with a walk to nearby public parks (Sondermarken and Frederiksberg) and the zoo, if you start early enough in the day.

Admission: Free.

Open: Tours given Mon–Fri at 11am and 2pm (call to confirm these hours). **Bus:** No. 6 from Town Hall Square.

TUBORG BREWERY, Strandvejen 54, Hellerup. Tel. 31/29-33-11, ext. 2212.

Carlsberg and Tuborg merged in 1970, but the two companies still maintain separate breweries and labels. Of the two tours, Tuborg's seems more authentic and homey as it winds its way through narrow passageways and refrigerators. The "Largest Beer Bottle in the World," holding the equivalent of about a million regular-size bottles of beer, is also on the premises. Like all good brewery tours, this one concludes with a sampling.

Eksperimentarium, an exciting new addition to the brewery housed in its old bottling hall, is a hands-on science and technology laboratory with "please touch" exhibits and special activities for children (tel. 39/27-33-33). Tuborg is a short S-tog ride to Ryparken, where you'll find the **Memorial Park,** dedicated to Danish civilians who lost their lives during the German occupation of Denmark from April 9, 1940, to May 5, 1945. Among the 158 graves are those of 31 people who died in concentration camps.

Admission: Free.

Open: Tours given Mon–Fri at 10am, 12:30pm, and 2:30pm (call to confirm these hours). **S-tog:** Hellerup.

SPECIAL & FREE EVENTS

Gråbrødre Torv, a square in the very center of Copenhagen, comes alive each summer day with street entertainers, outdoor cafés, and occasional live music concerts. Renovated in traditional Danish style, Gråbrødre Torv is a beautiful meeting place for people of all ages.

Nyhavn (the New Harbor), off Kongens Nytorv, is a dead-end canal lined by historic buildings and another summer favorite. Once the raucous sailors' quarter, Nyhavn has become an upscale strolling area lined with fairly expensive cafés and restaurants. During the summer the cafés lining Nyhavn's pedestrian streets appear to specialize in ice cream and beer. Majestic, tall, fully rigged ships are moored all along the canal, and you can also see where Hans Christian Andersen lived during different periods of his life—at nos. 18, 20, and 67 Nyhavn.

Nyhavn's wild maritime past is still evidenced by a couple of old-time bars (see "The Bar Scene" in Chapter 9) and tattoo parlors. **Tattoo Ole,** at Nyhavn 17, has been decorating bodies since 1862, and may be the oldest extant tattoo shop in the world.

6. SPORTS & RECREATION

SPECTATOR SPORTS

The main spectator sport in Copenhagen is watching the constantly changing scene along Strøget. If you had something more athletic in mind, do as the Danes do and support the national sport, soccer, by taking in a match at **Københavns Idrætspark,** Vedidrætspark 7 (tel. 31/42-68-60). The season is generally from late March to October.

RECREATION

If you're physically active at home and don't want to change your habits on the road, consider these possibilities. Should you need more information about sports or sporting organizations, check the "Sports" section of *Copenhagen This Week* or call **Idrættens Hus** at 42/45-55-55.

AEROBICS Check out studios and classes at **Scala,** Vesterbrogade 2E (tel. 33/32-10-02), and **Strøget,** Østergade 24A (tel. 33/93-00-29).

BICYCLES FOR FREE Since 1991, all you do is pay a refundable deposit of 20 Kr ($3.50) for the free use of a bike for city use only (it'll be just a basic model, mind you, not one built for speed). You can pick up or drop off bikes at one of 800 racks around town—that's one at almost every other street corner.

BICYCLE RENTALS Bikes may be rented at **Københavns Cyklebors,** at the west end of Central Station, Reventlowsgade 11 (tel. 33/14-07-17), or a couple of blocks away at **Dan Wheel,** Colbjørnsensgade 3 (tel. 31/21-22-27). Figure about 50 Kr ($8.80) a day for a three-speed, and increasingly less per day the longer you keep the bike, along with a 200 Kr ($35) refundable deposit.

For information about biking throughout Denmark, contact **Dansk Cyklist Forbund,** Kjeld Langes Gade 14 (tel. 33/32-31-21), Monday through Wednesday and Friday 9:30am to 3pm, Thursday until 6pm.

The **Danish State Railways (DSB)** rents bikes at the following stations: Klampenborg (tel. 31/64-08-60); Hillerød (tel. 32/25-51-86), Lyngby (tel. 32/87-02-65), Nykøbing F (tel. 33/85-02-44), and Næstved (tel. 33/72-01-40). Always call ahead to make sure bikes are available.

BOAT RENTALS Call **Danish Boat Charter** (tel. 31/63-08-00) and soon you'll be sailing on the Øresund on your own.

FISHING The following companies offer excursions of five to seven hours on the Øresund; they also rent tackle.

M/S *Hanne Berit*, Rungsted Havn, and **M/S *Antares*,** Helsingør (tel. for both 42/57-07-24 or 30/22-36-30).

M/S *Skipper*, Kalkbrænderihavnen (tel. 47/38-41-46 or 47/38-39-41). Departures daily; take the S-tog or bus no. 20 to Nordhavn.

M/S *Kastrup*, Kastrup Industrihavn (tel. 31/50-54-38). Daily departures; charters only on weekdays.

GOLF Arrangements to play at a course in North Zealand, including transportation, a guide, equipment rental, greens fee, and some sightseeing, may be made through **Dan Golf** (tel. 42/29-20-50). Or play at the 18-hole **Copenhagen Golf Club,** Eremitagen, Klampenborg (tel. 31/63-04-83 for information and booking); to get there, take the S-tog to Klampenborg.

HORSEBACK RIDING Horses may be hired by the hour or half hour at the **Sports Riding Club,** Maltegardsvej, Gentofte (tel. 31/65-17-02); rental hours are limited.

ICE SKATING The season lasts from October through March. These are two possibilities for an outing:

Herlev Ice Rink, 204 Tvedvangen, Herlev (tel. 42/84-68-20); take S-tog C to Herlev, then bus no. 167.

Østerbro Ice Rink, 6 Per Henrik Lings Allé (tel. 31/26-29-46); take bus no. 1, 6, or 14.

SQUASH The **Copenhagen Squash Club,** Vestersohus, Vester Sogade (tel. 33/11-86-38), rents courts, racquets, and balls.

SWIMMING The half-dozen open-air pools in the metropolitan Copenhagen area are open from mid-May through August; all are a bus or subway ride from the center. They include:

Baynehøj, 90 Enghavevej (tel. 31/21-49-00); take the S-tog to Sydhavn.

Bellahøj, 1–3 Bellahøjvej (tel. 31/60-16-66); take bus no. 5, 8, or 68. It's open weekdays from 7:30am to 7pm, weekends from 9am to 6pm.

Vestbad, Nørrekær, Brondbyoster (tel. 31/75-36-26); take S-tog B or bus no. 41.

Indoor pools with saunas are one of Copenhagen's best values, costing $3.50 or less. All are a bus ride from the center, so be sure to call and check opening and closing hours before you head out. They include:

Frederiksberg Swimming Baths, 29 Helgesvej (tel. 38/88-00-71); take bus no. 2 or 29.

Hillerødgade Baths, 35 Sandbjerggade (tel. 31/85-19-55); take bus no. 5, 7, 16, or 19.

Sundby Swimming Bath, 50 Sundbyvestervej (tel. 31/58-55-68); take bus no. 30, 32, 34, or 35.

Vesterbro Swimming Baths, 4 Angelgade (tel. 31/22-05-00); take bus no. 10.

TENNIS Advance bookings are necessary, no matter where you play. The most centrally located courts are in **Hotel Mercur,** 17 Vester Farimagsgade (tel. 33/12-57-11), within walking distance of Tivoli; nonguests may use them but pay a premium to do so.

There are also courts at two branches of **Københavns Boldklub,** Peter Bangsvej 147 (tel. 31/71-41-80), and Pile Allé 14 (tel. 31/30-23-00); take bus no. 1 to the first location, bus no. 28 or 41 to the second.

CHAPTER 7

STROLLING AROUND COPENHAGEN

You'll find yourself walking everywhere in Copenhagen. The streets brim with an energy and a momentum all their own, and the network of pedestrian thoroughfares draws you along in a mesmerizing way. The following walking tours take you past many points of interest. If you enjoy organized walking tours, **Copenhagen on Foot** offers many from late June to mid-October; the cost for most tours is 25 Kr ($4.40) for adults, 15 Kr ($2.65) for those ages 14 to 23.

WALKING TOUR 1 — Old City: From Town Hall to Kultorvet

Start: Town Hall Square.
Finish: Kultorvet.
Time: 3 hours.
Best Time: Anytime.

The first walking tour will take you down the narrow streets of Copenhagen that date back to the late 1300s, many now closed to traffic. The sights, smells, and sounds all compose a mosaic of a city that is both old and new. Begin at Town Hall Square, at Vesterbrogade and H. C. Andersens Boulevard. The square is a familiar landmark in Copenhagen, and within easy walking distance of the train station and the surrounding hotels. Directly in front of you is the striking:

1. **Town Hall,** built in 1905, only Copenhagen's sixth—not bad for a city that is nine centuries old. It boasts the city's highest tower at 348 feet. For clock lovers who don't mind the

admission fee, there's the gigantic **Jens Olsen's astronomical clock** just inside the building and to the right. A gilt statue of Bishop Absalon decorates the entry. And you can't miss the dramatic **Dragon Fountain** out front. Also take note of the unique:

2. **"Barometer tower,"** cattycorner from the fountain and a Copenhagen landmark in its own right. On sunny days the female figure of the tower ventures out with her bike; on cloudy days she is seen with her umbrella. From Town Hall Square, cross Vestervoldgade to set foot on:
3. **Strøget,** the world's longest pedestrian street. Here at Frederiksberggade at the west end of Strøget the shops are moderately priced and casual. As you proceed east (this tour encompasses about two-thirds of Strøget; Walking Tour 2 picks up the rest) the shops become ritzier. In its entirety, Strøget measures a mile in length. Meander along and enjoy the diversity of shops. After a couple of blocks you'll reach a large open square, which actually is two squares:
4. **Gammel Torv (Old Square),** to your left, is the oldest market square in Copenhagen, dating from the 15th century. It showcases the stately **Caritas Fountain,** the city's only remaining Dutch Renaissance well. It is easy to imagine people of olden times bringing their buckets and their horses here for water. And to your right is:
5. **Ny Torv (New Square),** a couple of centuries younger than Gammel Torv. For several hundred years, the old town hall, which burned in 1795, sat facing Gammel Torv in the spot where Strøget now intersects the two squares. It was replaced by the building on the southwest corner of Ny Torv, which was preempted by the present Town Hall and now serves as the city's **Courthouse (Domhuset).**

REFUELING STOP All along your way, you'll pass **fast-food vendors** selling pastries, ice cream, and souvlaki, as well as an **open-air market** with a variety of fruit. So if you're so inclined, you can snack as you cross town.

Continuing east, to your left you will notice:

6. **Holy Ghost Church (Helligandskirken),** set back from the street. Most of it was reconstructed after the fire of 1728; however, the wing to the right of the main sanctuary is more than 500 years old. This wing was once the hospital of the monastery of the Order of the Holy Ghost; and if it is open (as it occasionally is for an exhibition or book sale), take a peek inside at the vaulted ceiling and trim granite columns. A chapel of the

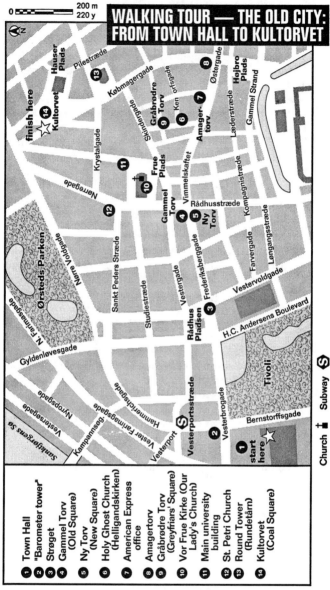

WALKING TOUR — THE OLD CITY: FROM TOWN HALL TO KULTORVET

1. Town Hall
2. "Barometer tower"
3. Strøget
4. Gammel Torv (Old Square)
5. Ny Torv (New Square)
6. Holy Ghost Church (Helligandskirken)
7. American Express office
8. Amagertorv
9. Gråbrødre Torv (Greyfriars' Square)
10. Vor Frue Kirke (Our Lady's Church)
11. Main university building
12. St. Petri Church
13. Round Tower (Rundetårn)
14. Kultorvet (Coal Square)

church is open to people of all religious persuasions for meditation. Just behind the church is a popular Italian restaurant that serves a value-packed buffet daily, **Pasta Basta.**

At the end of this block of Strøget is the:

7. American Express office, at the corner of Niels

Hemmingsens Gade. From here to the east end of Strøget you're going to encounter some of the best street entertainers in the world. My favorites are the mainly classical duo of Jens Erik Raasted on flute and Gernold Schonenberg on guitar. Proceed along Strøget to:

8. **Amagertorv,** an open square that during medieval times bustled as a marketplace. Its centerpiece is the unique **Stork Fountain;** on the queen's birthday and other special occasions, "golden" apples bob on the sprays of water. Amagertorv garners its share of street performers—musicians, choirs, clowns, and jugglers. The Dutch Renaissance–style house at **No. 6** (1606) is now owned by **Royal Copenhagen** and houses the firm's showrooms and an elegant café. The **tobacconist** has been ensconced at **No. 9** since 1864 (see the little museum inside).

REFUELING STOP If you have a sweet tooth—and who doesn't—drop into **Restaurant Amagertorv** in the Royal Copenhagen building—on the third floor—and order the *kartoffel* (potato) cake, a custard-filled cream puff generously decorated with marzipan and dusted with cocoa.

Turn off Strøget at this juncture, and head north (to your left) on the twisting Købmagergade, a wide pedestrian street that was a major thoroughfare in olden times. At the narrow Lovstræde, turn left. It quickly leads to:

9. **Gråbrødre Torv (Greyfriars' Square),** the sheltered heart of the Old City and one of the city's best-concealed secrets (from visitors, anyway). It's dear to Copenhageners of all ages, who love to sit under the old plane tree and wile away a summer day. The square was named after a Franciscan monastery that stood here during the Middle Ages, and the houses around it date from 1730.

REFUELING STOP Hungry for an American-style burger or omelet? **Sporevejen** is the place, with all the grandeur of a New Jersey diner. For a drink and more upscale (that is, trendy) atmosphere, go to the basement bar at **Peder Oxe Vinkælder.** Both are on the square.

If you can wrest yourself away from the haven of tranquility that Gråbrødre Torv provides, turn left onto Skindergade to pick up the pedestrian street **Fiolstræde,** known for its used-book shops, as far as **Frue Plads** and:

10. **Vor Frue Kirke (Our Lady's Church),** a neoclassical cathedral built in 1829. It may be the cathedral, but it's not the city's most memorable church architecturally. However, inside there are marble statues of the Twelve Apostles and, at the altar, the acclaimed statue of Christ, all by noted Danish sculptor Bertel Thorvaldsen. Beside the cathedral is the:
11. **main university building**—built between 1831 and 1836—which now houses administrative offices. The university itself was founded much earlier in 1479 by Christian I; its architectural style, adopted in the 19th century, was influenced by English universities. The surrounding area, known as the Latin Quarter, is filled with young students, bohemian coffeehouses, and—as one would expect—used-book stores. Across Nørregade is:
12. **St. Petri Church,** a German house of worship built in 1450. The tower was added in 1757. The old cemetery is accessible from Skt. Peders Stræde. Follow the pedestrian street **Store Kannikestræde** back to Købmagergade and you find yourself face-to-face with the:
13. **Round Tower,** a well-loved city landmark attached to Trinity Church. Built as an observatory as well as the church's tower—an inspired stroke of creativity and practicality—this is the tower referred to in Hans Christian Andersen's story "The Tinder Box." A bust of Tycho Brahe, the 16th-century Danish astronomer, stands outside. For a small admission charge, you can climb the steep spiral ramp (no steps) to the top. Halfway up the tower, you'll pass a gallery that features interesting exhibits (free). At the summit, you are rewarded with a splendid view of the old town and a panorama of Copenhagen. Legend has it that Peter the Great, on a state visit to Denmark, galloped up the ramp on horseback, followed by his czarina in a horse-drawn carriage. After you leave the Round Tower, continue north on Købmagergade to:
14. **Kultorvet (Coal Square).** In centuries past, vendors sold charcoal here. Now there are lots of shops to browse, including the excellent **UFF,** at nos. 9 and 13, for secondhand clothing. If you want to work your way back to Strøget from here either follow the pedestrian walkway **Fiolstræde,** or take the S-tog only two blocks away at **Nørreport station**—where the northern gate to the Old City used to be—to your next destination.

A FINAL REFUELING STOP At Kultorvet, drop into **Klaptræet** café for inexpensive, light fare and unstudied bohemian atmosphere. If you haven't brought a book or magazine—as reading seems the appropriate thing to do here—read the walls. Afterward, take in a flick; a movie theater featuring avant-garde films is right upstairs.

WALKING TOUR 2 — Old City: From Strædet to Nyhavn

Start: The Lur Blowers statue, on the east side of Town Hall.
Finish: Kongens Nytorv.
Time: 2 hours.
Best Time: Anytime.

On this second walking tour, you will amble down a lesser-known and, naturally, less crowded pedestrian street, Strædet—actually an amalgam of several streets: Farvergade, Kompagnistræde, and Læderstræde. Collectors will love this district, known for its antique shops, galleries, and antiquarian bookshops. The walking tour begins at the:

1. **Lur Blowers Statue,** on a pedestal on the east side of Town Hall. This statue depicts two musicians playing lurs, ancient instruments resembling trumpets. Found only in Scandinavia—more than 30 in Denmark alone—lurs are 5 to 6 feet in length and are believed to date back 3,000 years. Eighteen lurs are on display at the National Museum, where you can hear a recording of their sound. Cross the street and proceed along Farvergade, the beginning of Strædet. After one block it becomes Kompagnistræde, which you should follow one block to Rådhustræde. Cross Rådhustræde, turn right, and walk down to no. 13, the address of:
2. **Huset,** a building set back off the street (its name means "the house"). Unique to Copenhagen, and the envy of any city that cares about providing an inviting meeting place for its youth, it houses a student information center, video gallery, bar, café, and disco. The information clearinghouse on the second floor has wonderful maps and a friendly staff, and it's a great place to meet other travelers. From Huset, retrace your steps to Kompagnistræde and proceed along Strædet at leisure. This is a great street for window shopping, lined with **antiques shops** displaying every conceivable collectible. Strædet deadends into:
3. **Højbro Plads,** a large square best known for the **equestrian statue of Bishop Absalon,** which will be to your right. The

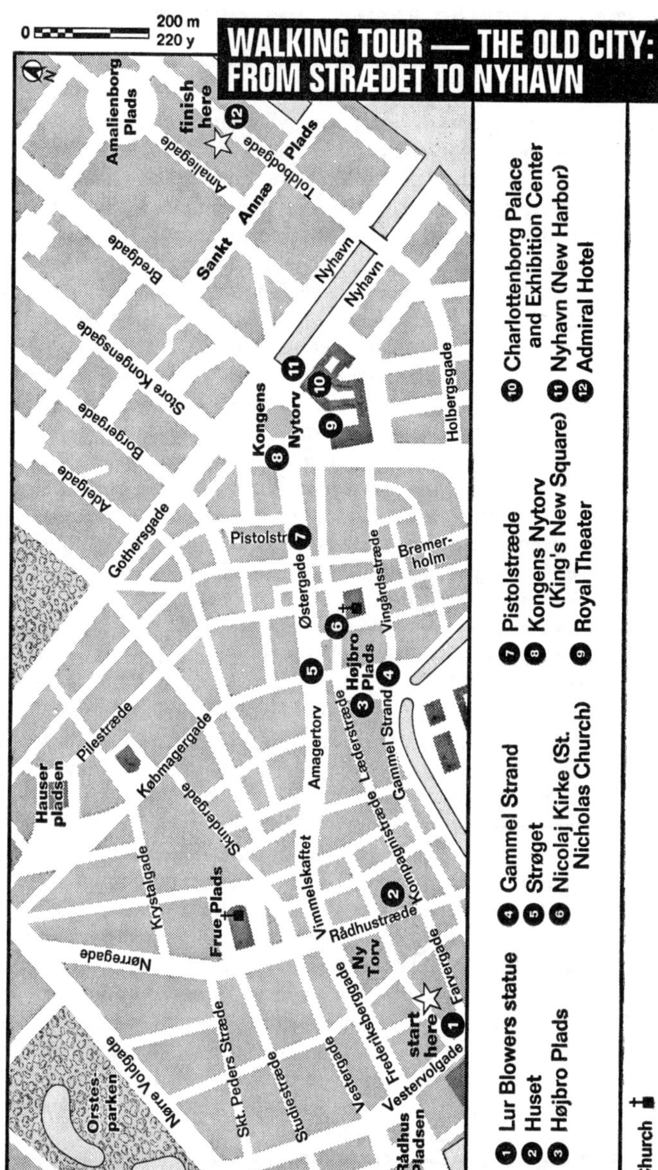

steeple rising behind the statue belongs to St. Nicholas Church (see no. 6 below). From this vantage point, there is a good view of **Slotsholmen (Castle Island),** home to the **Thorvaldsen Museum** and **Christiansborg Castle** with its solid, crown-capped spire. Christiansborg houses the Danish parliament, supreme court, and the queen's reception rooms. The canal flowing directly in front of you is:

4. **Gammel Strand,** site of the city's oldest port and now a point of departure for canal tours. Only a few decades ago, fishing boats used to haul their catch of the day here to be sold at a then bustling market. Today a granite statue of a lone **Fisherwoman** standing by the water's edge commemorates that earlier time. From Højbro Plads, head one block north to:
5. **Strøget,** the city's famous mile-long pedestrian street, and turn right onto it. You'll pick it up at Østergade (East Street) and proceed along the most elegant third of it (the majority of Strøget is described in Walking Tour 1). Upscale **Illums** department store is at Østergade 52 (take a quick peek at the atrium; there are telephones and rest rooms on the lower level). To your right, and a stone's throw from Strøget, is:
6. **Nicolaj Kirke (St. Nicholas Church).** The existing structure was completed in 1914, but its square brick tower has held its ground here since the Middle Ages; the church is no longer used for religious services but houses exhibitions, concerts, and a small but overpriced café.

REFUELING STOP A *Frommer* reader turned me on to **American Pizza,** just behind St. Nicholas Church, at the corner of Vingardestræde. In a laid-back, inviting atmosphere, there's a scrumptious pizza buffet, moderately priced. If you're not hungry, perhaps you'd like a soft drink or beer before continuing your tour.

At Østergade 15 is the **Holmegaard Glassworks,** with its exquisite crystal, practical and decorative; and at no. 3, the **Bang & Olufsen Center,** a must for anyone interested in top-quality audio/video equipment (the equipment is showcased in a shop called **Fredgaard** at no. 26). Near the end of Strøget, and to your left, is a splinter of a street called:

7. **Pistolstræde,** whose houses and courtyard have been turned into trendy shops and restaurants, the "yuppiest" part of Copenhagen. A quick walk-through, followed by a sharp right on Ny Østergade, will bring you back to Strøget, which ends (or begins, to be perfectly honest) at:
8. **Kongens Nytorv (King's New Square)** with an **equestrian statue of Christian V,** at its center. To your left is **Hotel d'Angleterre,** Copenhagen's dowager hotel, and beyond it **Magasin du Nord,** the largest department store in Scandinavia, a former hotel itself. At the southern end of the square is the:
9. **Royal Theater,** founded in 1748 and a showcase for dance,

operatic, and theatrical productions. Across the street from the theater, continuing in counterclockwise fashion around the square, is the:

10. **Charlottenborg Palace and Exhibition Center,** home to the Danish Academy of Fine Arts. Young artists and designers show their work here. The interior is quite elegant and worth a glimpse.

REFUELING STOPS At Kongens Nytorv, you can take your pick: the legendary *conditori* **La Glace** for pastries; the historic wine cellar **Hviids Vinstue,** at no. 19; or **Cafe Dan Turrell,** the popular student haunt for chili and a beer—only a couple of blocks from the square at Store Regnegade 3–5.

Continue making your way around Kongens Nytorv until you see an oversized **anchor,** a memorial to Danish sailors who died in World War II. This marks the beginning of:

11. **Nyhavn (New Harbor),** the formerly sleazy sailor's quarter is now squeaky clean by comparison and unabashedly picturesque. Upscale restaurants fill most of the row houses, but you can still find a remaining sailor's bar (no. 17, for instance) and tattoo parlor (also no. 17). **Hans Christian Andersen** lived and wrote many of his fairy tales in Nyhavn, at nos. 18, 20, and 67. If architectural adaptations interest you, take a look inside the:
12. **Admiral Hotel** (formerly a warehouse) only a couple of blocks from Nyhavn at Toldbodgade 24–28. This hotel is a unique example of architectural recycling.

FINAL REFUELING STOP Toast "Wonderful Copenhagen" with a glass of champagne at **Nyhavns Færgro,** at Nyhavn 5.

WALKING TOUR 3 — The Little Mermaid & Citadel Park

Start: Gefion Fountain.
Finish: Fight for Freedom Museum.
Time: 1½ hours.
Best Time: The morning is preferable for the nice light, and there are fewer bus-tour groups milling around The Little Mermaid.

When trolls venture outside Norway, they probably come to wander the wooded lanes around the Citadel (at night, of course, which we won't do). This tour covers a lot of territory, from the touristic to the tranquil, in a short amount of time, but you can stretch it out as long as you like if you pack a picnic lunch. Begin the tour at the monumental:

1. **Gefion Fountain,** which illustrates the legend of the founding of Denmark. A goddess was given a very short time to dig land out of Sweden that would become Denmark; so to accomplish her task, she turned her two sons into oxen and plowed like hell. Visible through the fountain's spray is:
2. **St. Albans Church,** also known as the English Church. Walk up the steps behind the fountain and along the walkway (you'll most likely be carried along by the crowd) that leads to:
3. **The Little Mermaid (Den Lille Havfrue),** the endearing symbol of Copenhagen. Her wistful look makes you want to put your arm around her and comfort her, although she's perched on a stone at the harbor's edge and you can't reach her. She may be depressed by the unsightly freighters that mar her (and our) view. Her expression reminds me of a traveler who's been on the road too long without news from home, although in the fairy tale what she wants most is to leave home and explore the world. From the statue, take the paved walkway to:
4. **Citadel (Kastellet) Park,** a fortification that has been entrenched here since 1629. Cross the road and enter. Now you have a choice: to explore the ancient city ramparts by taking the **high road,** which offers pretty vistas and brings you quite close to a windmill, or the **low road,** which is easier to exit should you tire easily (I'd vote high).

   When you enter the park, the low road is immediately to your right; the high road is to the left (you'll walk through a covered passageway; from here, turn immediately to your right and go uphill).

   The Citadel itself dates from 1663 and is still surrounded by its original ramparts; you're walking on them. It is owned and used by the **Ministry of Defense,** so don't be surprised to see young soldiers doing drills. Most of the park is open to the public, and although you may feel a little like a trespasser, you're most welcome here.

   If you're on the low road and want to exit, a possible choice is at Grønningen and Folke Bernadottes, a block from the Østerport S-tog station. On the high road, you have to keep going; soon you'll see a near-extinct sight in a city, a **windmill** (get out your camera; it's a beauty).

   The high road exit appears soon after you glimpse a bridge and the spire of St. Albans Church. Take the left fork in the road,

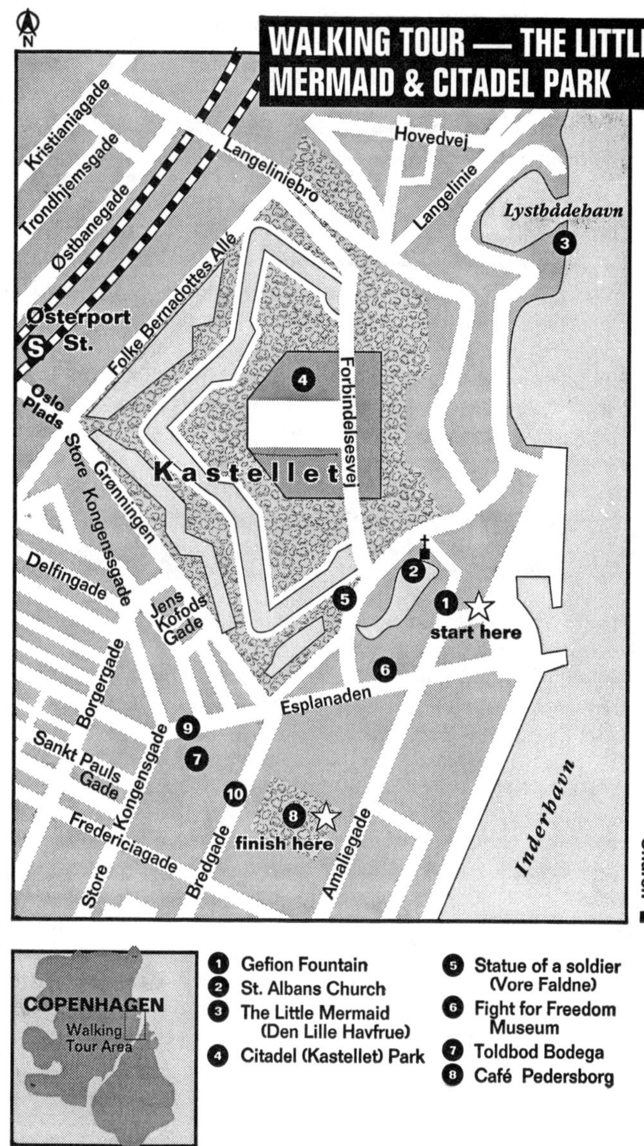

which will bring you down from your lofty vantage point to a cobblestone walkway. Turn right and cross the bridge to come out of the park. On your right will be the:

5. **Statue of a Soldier** *(Vore Faldne)*, whose presence here commemorates those who died during the years 1940 to 1945.

This memorial is quite evocative before a visit to the:

6. **Fight for Freedom Museum.** En route to it you'll pass a **bust of Winston Churchill** in **Churchill Park.** Sir Winston is looking down—for his cigar, the Danes claim. This bit of Britishness on Danish soil pays tribute to the country that freed Denmark from Nazi occupation in 1945. (There's a rest room here, should you need one.)

REFUELING STOP You may have worked up a thirst or an appetite by now, since this tour so far has passed no eateries or watering holes along the way. Lucky for you, there are two popular local cafés in the vicinity: the rustic **7. Toldbod Bodega,** at Esplanaden 4, and the slightly more formal **8. Café Pedersborg,** at Bredgade 76. Both serve typical Danish fare.

WALKING TOUR 4 — Christianshavn & Christiania

Start: The Stock Exchange at Holmens Canal.
Finish: Amagerbrogade and Torvegade.
Time: 3 hours (2 hours if you're not prone to gazing at length at scenic spots and buildings of architectural note).
Best Time: Anytime.

Christianshavn (Christian's Harbor) was the dream child of Christian IV, the Builder King, who foresaw an active shipping and trading community separate from Copenhagen (as indeed it was for many years). Shipyards, warehouses, and homes were built (and boomed) here in the 1700s. Christianshavn—built in the Dutch style with canals, giving it the feel of a "little Amsterdam"—was also meant to protect Copenhagen from an attack by sea. Today, the shipyards are quiet, the old warehouses have been converted into offices and enviably large apartments, and the only attacks on Copenhagen (invasions of tourists in summer) are welcome. Begin the tour in front of the:

1. **Stock Exchange (Bourse),** a Renaissance building erected on Slotsholmen from 1619 to 1640 by Christian IV. Take note of the spire, four dragon tails twisted together. Walk or take bus no. 2 one stop across the:
2. **Knippel's Bridge** (named after a Mr. Knip) into Christianshavn. The church at the west end of Strandgade is:
3. **Christianskirken (Christian's Church),** built from 1755 to 1759. Don't let its classical spire in the rococo style fool you; its unique interior is designed like a theater, complete with boxes in three tiers.

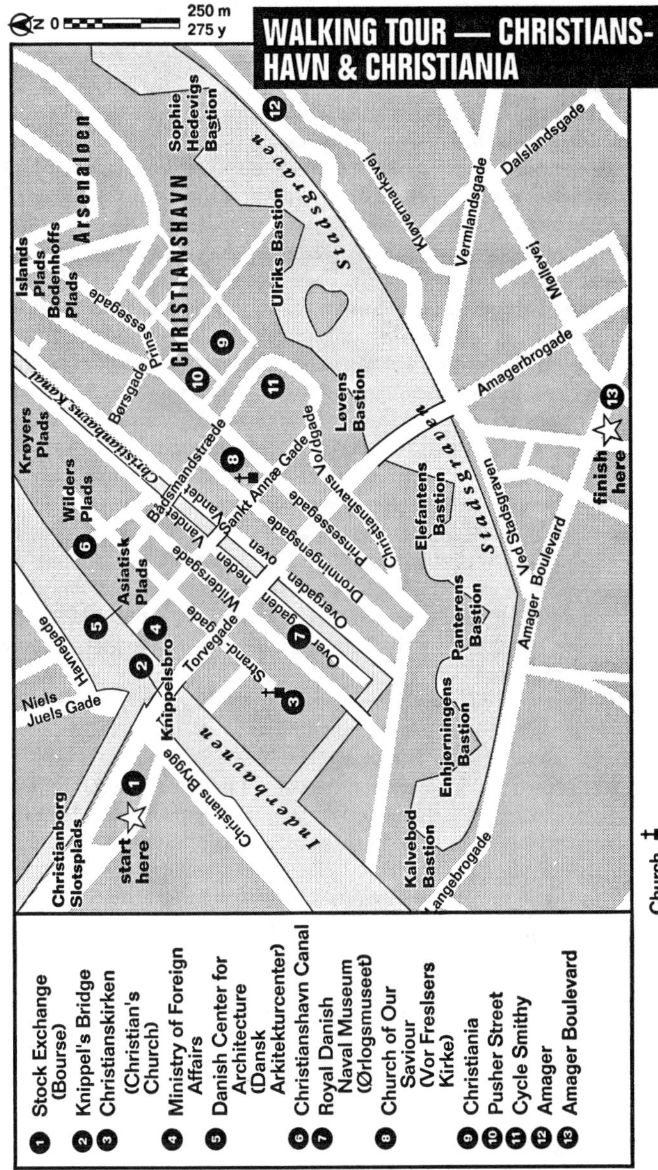

Walk east along Strandgade (away from the church). You'll pass merchants' houses from the 15th and 16th centuries, as well as the:

4. Ministry of Foreign Affairs, on your left, a large building that once belonged to the Asiatic Company, a major shipping concern in the 18th century, as well as the:

5. **Danish Center for Architecture (Dansk Arkitekturcenter),** also on the left, which has changing exhibits on modern Danish architecture. Continue along Strandgade to the:
6. **Christianshavn Canal,** one of Copenhagen's most charming and unsung spots. The restaurant at the water's edge, called **The Canal,** is yummy but costly. From here there is a good view of Christian's Church (no. 3 above).

   Retrace your steps along Strandgade to Sankt Annæ Gade and turn left. The view of the canal and Christianshavn from the small **bridge at Overgaden Oven Vandet** is cause for pause, cameras in hand. On this tiny street, you'll also find the:
7. **Royal Danish Naval Museum (Orlogsmuseet),** at no. 58, housed in a former naval hospital. It's open every afternoon except Monday, and showcases 300 models of ships, the oldest from 1687, as well as other maritime memorabilia. (If you visit the museum, make your way back to Sankt Annæ Gade.)

REFUELING STOP **Café Wilder,** a local favorite—one of mine, too—at Wildersgade 56 and Sankt Annæ Gade, serves fresh light fare. You could sit with a cup of coffee here for hours and no one would hurry you. If it's too early in the tour to stop now, consider coming back here at the end of the tour or some other time.

Follow Sankt Annæ Gade to the:

8. **Church of Our Saviour (Vor Freslsers Kirke),** built in 1682, with its unique spiral steeple. It's possible to climb the 400 spiraling steps for a magnificent view of Copenhagen. Atop the tower, a gilt figure of Christ stands on the earth. At the end of this block, turn left and follow Prinsessgade past Badsmandesstræde to the main entrance (a big gate) to:
9. **Christiania,** the counterculture community that gained notoriety in the early seventies. It's still notorious. The two-story brick building on your right houses a gallery with changing exhibits (open daily from noon to 5pm), as well as a jazz club called **Loppen,** and a restaurant called **Spiseloppen.** A good map of Christiania in the gallery will help you get your bearings—and you will need help here as nothing is marked. Rest rooms are on the top floor of the building.

   You may be put off by the ambience of Christiania—especially **10. Pusher Street,** the community's main street where the taking of photographs is not appreciated. In other areas it's more acceptable; just remember that people, some 900 of them, make their homes here, albeit in a place that has always been a public curiosity.

Proceed to the end of Pusher Street to where the green house is, and turn left.

Walk two blocks, passing the **11. Cycle Smithy.** Go in and have a look at the unique Copenhagen Pedersen bicycle—known locally as the "Christiania bike." At the end of this block, turn right and follow the path that leads past houses along the water.

Cross the **bridge** (a nice spot for photos) to the island of:

12. Amager and follow the footpath to your right. You'll pass colorful, innovative homes—quite comfortable on the inside and heated by wood-burning stoves in winter. When you get to the **large brick structure,** you may walk around it or go through the yard if you sense you won't be intruding.

From here, follow the **path by the water,** it's prettier than the one to your left. But stay alert; it's also a busy bike path, frequented by a Christiania-esque mode of transport: a large tricycle with a box in front for transporting goods and children. When steps appear to the left, climb them for a glimpse of orderly little houses across a sliver of a canal. Return to the lower path for a lovely view of the spiral tower of the Church of Our Savior.

Either path will lead to **13. Amager Boulevard,** the main street of Amager, at the cross section of Torvegade, the main traffic artery on Christianshavn. You have just crossed from one world into another.

On Amager Boulevard, take bus no. 30, 33, or 34 to Town Hall Square. Or, if you're not ready to give up the tranquility here, take the small bridge that was on your left as you exited the path and stroll past some of those tidy Amager houses lining the little canal. Or you can hotfoot it back to Café Wilder.

CHAPTER 8

SHOPPING A TO Z

Shopping in Copenhagen begins on **Strøget,** the address of many of the city's most exclusive stores: **Royal Copenhagen, Bing & Grondahl, Georg Jensen, Holmegaard,** the upscale department store **Illums,** and the home-furnishings specialty store, **Illums Bolighus.** Fashionable **Magasin du Nord,** at Kongens Nytorv opposite the Royal Theater, is the largest department store in Scandinavia; this stately French Renaissance building was formerly the Hotel du Nord, where Hans Christian Andersen was a celebrated guest.

Parallel to (and a block south of) Strøget, another pedestrian street, called **Strædet,** is well known for its antiques stores, antiquarian bookshops, and galleries. Perpendicular to Strøget and branching north to the Nørreport S-tog is **Købmagergade,** also blessedly free of cars. Several other city shopping streets are reserved exclusively for pedestrians and are marked in red on most tourist maps. **Gammel Kongevej** and **Vesterbrogade,** in the western part of the city, are filled with shops where you might find better bargains than along the more heavily trafficked shopping streets. To explore them, walk out along the one, back along the other.

Two favorites for top-quality secondhand clothing are **Kvindehuset** (Women's House), Gothersgade 37, only open noon to 6pm weekdays, and the well-stocked **UFF** at Kultorvet 13 (come here for jeans). Other fertile hunting grounds are the streets framed by **Vestervoldgade, Nørre Voldgade, Nørregade,** and **Vestergade.**

By no means overlook the **museum shops** (the one at the National Museum has unusual, striking jewelry modeled on Viking amulets) and the outstanding selection of **duty-free** and **specialty shops**—about 30 in all—at the **Copenhagen Airport.**

BEST BUYS

Copenhagen is known for its crystal, porcelain, pewter, jewelry, toys, furniture, home furnishings, lighting, audiovideo equipment, and down comforters (called *dyner)*—not necessarily cheap but excellent value for the quality and craftsmanship. Since the Danes like to entertain at home, and comfortable furnishings and good lighting are important to them, stores stock extensive selections, including bookshelves, since the Danes tend to be great readers. Simple items like candles and baskets are available for less than you would pay at home.

While I'm a budget traveler in thought, deed, and pocketbook, I'll splurge on a souvenir long before I will on a fancy dinner out. A special purchase from a place I love is something I treasure over the years. For example, two Holmegaard schnapps glasses I bought in 1987 (they were all I could afford) always give me immense pleasure whenever I use them, so much so that I bought two more on a visit several years later. (I think a tradition has been inaugurated.)

If I don't have much money to spare on shopping, I happily make do with postcards, museum prints, or a cassette or CD of music from the place. But I still visit the upscale shops (many are included below) to admire the craftsmanship and to make mental notes about what I'll buy on my return, when I have more money.

Major sales are held in Copenhagen in August and January, but you'll find sale signs and bins with special discounts all year through.

Many stores will ship purchases home for you, which is convenient for two reasons: You don't have to lug them around (in the case of furniture, it's impossible anyway), and you avoid paying the VAT (see below). On the other hand, you do have to pay a shipping charge.

STORE HOURS

Stores generally are open Monday through Thursday from 9:30am to 5:30pm, on Friday until 7pm, and on Saturday from 9:30am to 1pm. Note that on Monday some shops don't open until 10am, and many bakeries don't open at all.

TAXES & REFUNDS

All purchases are subject to a 22% **valued-added tax (VAT)**, called MOMS in Denmark, but many stores offer non-EEC and non-Scandinavian citizens the chance to recover it on purchases of 600 Kr ($105.25) or more. (Scandinavians and citizens of EEC countries must make much heftier purchases—1,200 and 3,100 Kr, respectively.) To get the VAT back, ask for white and green copies of the tax-free invoice (the green will be your receipt). Present the white copy with the *unopened* purchase when you leave the country, and the money (minus a 5% service charge) will be refunded in one of four ways: in cash (your choice of half a dozen currencies, including U.S. dollars), in a check mailed to your home address, a reimbursement to your credit card, or a deposit in a Danish bank account.

If you leave by plane from 8am to 4pm, have the invoice stamped at Customs Services in the departure hall of the airport (if you depart between 4pm and 8am, go to the arrival hall, which is

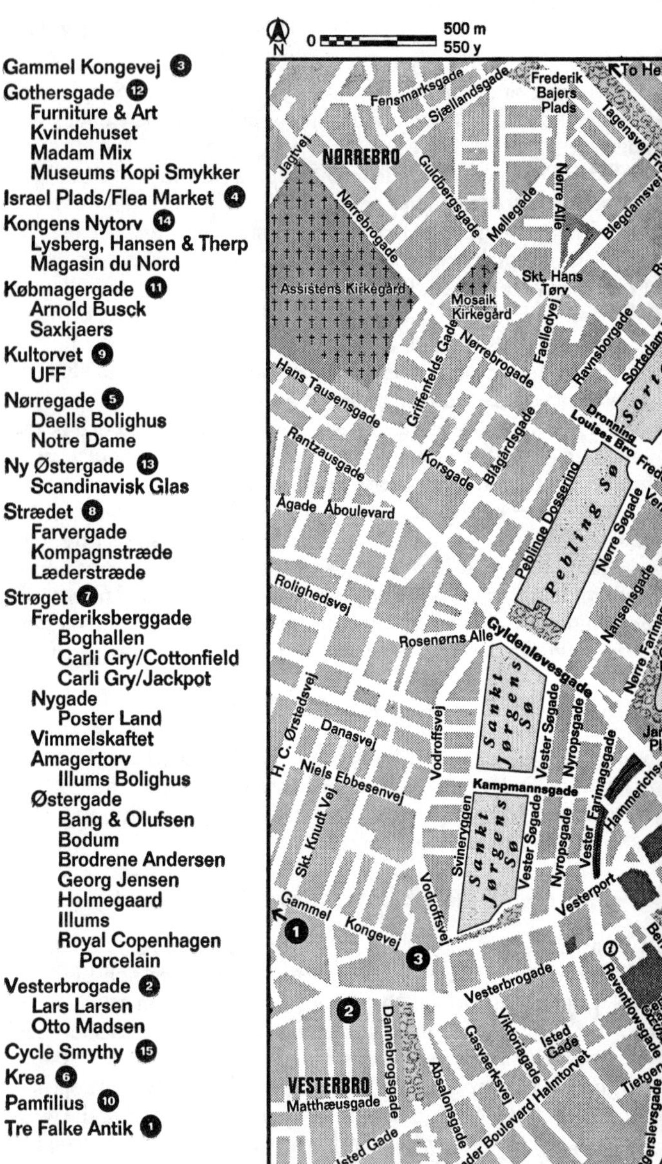

adjacent to the departure hall). You then submit the stamped invoice and the merchandise to the Refund Office in the transit hall (turn left after you pass the security check); the office is open daily from 7am to 10pm. If you don't want to wait for a cash reimbursement, leave the paperwork in the box outside the office and the refund will be mailed to you (a much longer wait in the long run).

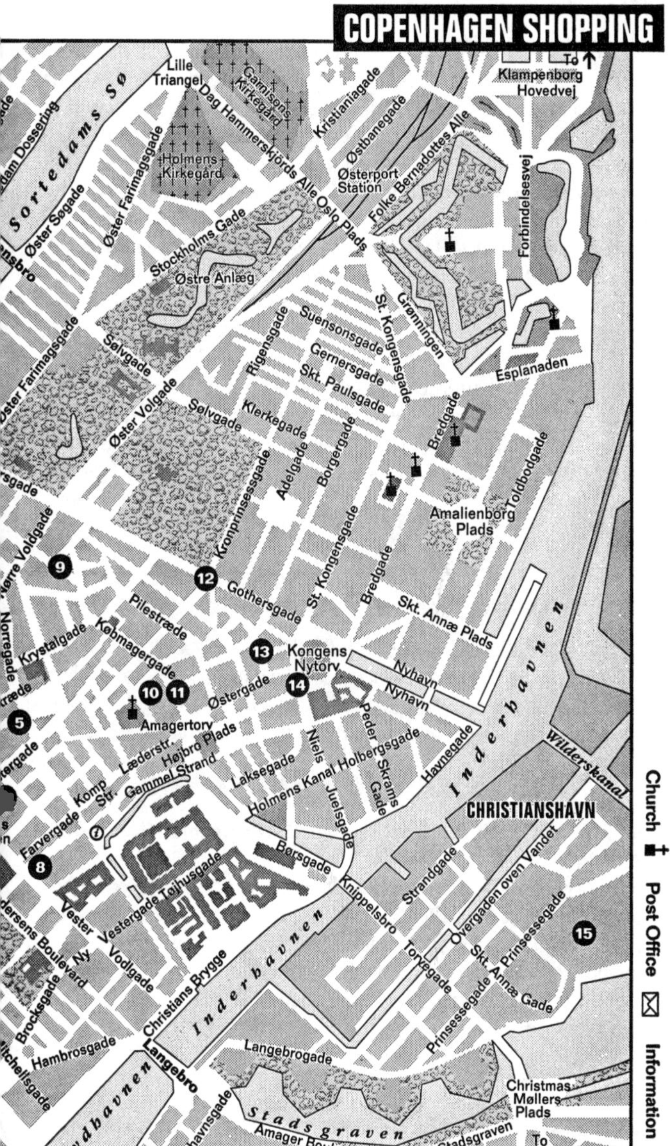

If you leave by train, contact a ticket collector at the last station before leaving the country, show your merchandise, and have the invoice stamped. (I'd recommend double-checking this at the train station in Copenhagen—not waiting until the eleventh hour, as it were.) Then send the invoice to Danish Tax-Free Shopping for a refund.

If you leave by ship, contact a Customs agent at the Port of Copenhagen (tel. 31/26-08-41); the office is open 24 hours a day. When you go there, bring the purchase as well as the invoice. If you sail from another Danish city, contact a Customs agent before departing Copenhagen.

If you leave by car, contact a Customs agent at the place where you leave the country, show the merchandise, get the invoice stamped, and send it to Danish Tax-Free Shopping, Pilegarden, H. J. Holstvej 5A, DK-2605 Brondby, Denmark.

If you failed to get the Customs stamp before leaving Denmark, there is still a chance to get a refund on the tax: Send Danish Duty-Free Shopping either a stamped official declaration from a country you visited after leaving Denmark confirming that the goods purchased in Denmark are being taken with you to the United States, or a declaration by the Danish consulate or Danish embassy in the United States that the goods indeed arrived in the United States.

ANTIQUES

Browse the multitude of shops on the pedestrian street **Strædet,** just south of Strøget, for a wide assortment of antiques.

TRE FALKE ANTIK, Falconer Allé 10. Tel. 31/24-18-46.

This tiny place in Frederiksberg, owned and managed by collector Connie Nordencrone, is filled with carefully selected treasures: antique clothing, silver jewelry, rhinestones, and Holmegaard crystal.

AUDIO/VIDEO EQUIPMENT

BANG & OLUFSEN, Østergade 3 (Strøget). Tel. 33/13-60-80.

World-class equipment is on view in their store at the east end of Strøget, almost at Kongens Nytorv. You may also see the equipment in home displays at a shop called Fredsgaard, down the street at Østergade 26. Products come with a worldwide service guarantee. If you don't get to admire them here, check the Museum of Modern Art in New York, but they won't be for sale.

BICYCLES

CYCLE SMITHY, in Christiania. Tel. 31/57-00-37.

Bicycle connoisseurs, consider the triangulated, cantilever-frame Copenhagen Pedersen, which sells for about 2,200 Kr ($386).

BOOKS

BOGHALLEN, Rådhuspladsen 37. Tel. 33/11-85-11.

In the Politiken building and a block from Town Hall and Strøget, this busy shop is well stocked with volumes about the history and culture of Copenhagen and Denmark, as well as the translated works of well-known Danish authors.

ARNOLD BUSCK, Købmagergade 49. Tel. 33/12-24-53.

You'll find a good selection in English in most every category. Paperbacks, fiction and nonfiction, range in price from 49 to 99 Kr ($8.60 to $17.35).

CHINA, SILVER & GLASS

HOLMEGAARD, Østergade 15. Tel. 31/12-44-77.

Famous for its glass and crystal, Holmegaard is housed in the oldest building in Østergard, the more-than-300-year-old Karel van Manders mansion, named after the royal court artist who lived here in the 17th century. A large selection of glasses, vases, bowls, and art objects is on the ground floor, but don't stop here; visit the glass lamps in the basement and the special exhibitions in Glasgalleriet (the Glass Gallery) on the second floor.

ROYAL COPENHAGEN PORCELAIN, Østergade 15. Tel. 31/12-44-77.

Three floors of this Renaissance building from 1616 house a large collection of Royal Copenhagen porcelain that includes dinnerware and hand-painted porcelain figurines and vases. The minimuseum displays works from the dawn of porcelain production. In summer, porcelain-painting demonstrations are given. An elegant café is on the premises.

SCANDINAVISK GLAS, Ny Østergade 4. Tel. 33/13-80-95.

Tucked behind the Hotel d'Angleterre, this lovely store features not only Royal Copenhagen and Swedish glassware from Orrefors and Kosta Boda, but Baccarat, Lalique, Lladró, Waterford, Hummel, and Wedgwood.

COMFORTERS

LARS LARSEN, Vesterbrogade.

You'll see down comforters in a number of fashionable downtown shops and in department stores, but this company manages to sell them at lower-than-average prices, and it's worth the walk or bus ride to have a look.

DEPARTMENT STORES

DAELL'S VAREHUS, Nørregade 12. Tel. 31/12-78-25.

The K-Mart of Copenhagen, what it lacks in elegance, it makes up for in bargains. Copenhageners shop here with good reason.

ILLUMS, Østergade 52 (Strøget). Tel. 33/14-40-02.

Ideally situated in the center of Strøget, this upscale store draws shoppers like a magnet. Be sure to peek inside at the marble atrium with its chandeliers and fountain.

MAGASIN DU NORD, Kongens Nytorv 13. Tel. 33/11-44-33.

In a striking Renaissance building that used to house the Hotel du Nord, this is Scandinavia's largest department store—a very elegant one at that.

FACTORY TOURS

HOLMEGAARD, Fensmark. Tel. 53/74-62-00.

Besides mining its Glass Shop for treasures, take a look in the museum, where old and new glassware is displayed. Refreshments are available at the Glass Inn. The factory, which has been here since 1825, is 80km (50 miles) southwest of Copenhagen and reachable by train to Næstved and then bus 7km (4.3 miles) to Fensmark. The bus stop is 105 yards from the factory door.

ROYAL COPENHAGEN PORCELAIN FACTORY, 45 Smallegade, Frederiksberg. Tel. 31/86-48-48.

Guided tours in English take place at 9, 10, and 11am.

FASHIONS

Stroll **Strøget** from one end to the other and you're bound to find something that speaks to your taste and pocketbook. Here are some favorites, on and off "The Street."

MEN'S

BRODRENE ANDERSEN, Østergade 7 (Strøget). Tel. 33/15-15-77.

One of Copenhagen's most fashionable men's stores, Andersen Brothers is also one of its oldest, founded in 1850. If you can't afford a suit, then a tie or a scarf perhaps.

CARLI GRY/COTTONFIELD, Frederiksberggade 12 (Strøget). Tel. 33/13-66-06.

Sharing a space with Jackpot, its companion shop (see below), Cottonfield, which is upstairs, features casual, comfortable clothing and accessories for men.

WOMEN'S

CARLI GRY/JACKPOT, Frederiksberggade 12. Tel. 33/13-66-06.

Stylish and fun clothing for women. The shop also carries nice costume jewelry. A second store is at Købmagergade 11.

SWEATERS

OTTO D. MADSEN, Vesterbrogade 1. Tel. 33/13-41-10.

If you want to take home authentic Scandinavian sweaters, in assorted styles and sizes for men and women, there are hundreds to choose from here, priced at least 100 Kr ($17.55) less than most places, especially at the airport. The store is in the arcade opposite Town Hall.

SECONDHAND CLOTHING

MADAM MIX, Store Regnegade 19 A-B at Gothersgade. Tel. 33/91-51-01.

If your taste runs toward funky, run toward this place.

KVINDEHUSET, Gothersgade 37. Tel. 33/93-38-70.

A small but well-chosen selection of fashions for women; some of the jackets, handmade from quilts, are quite distinctive.

UFF, Kultorvet 9 and 13. Tel. 31/16-64-07.

Denmark's answer to Good Will, these shops are well stocked with clothing in great condition. There are numerous locations; the two above are centrally located, with good selections, especially for jeans at no. 13. Fairly central locations include Nørrebrogade 54 and Vesterbrogade 37.

FOOD

See **Illums,** under "Department Stores."

GIFTS

PAMFILIUS, Valkendorfsgade 19. Tel. 33/93-93-57.

Just off Strøget and a block from the American Express office, this small, unassuming shop is a rich source of reasonably priced gifts and what-nots, as well as jewelry and dresses. It's tucked off the main drag, so many visitors don't discover it until they've spent all their money elsewhere; don't be so unfortunate.

FURNITURE & HOME FURNISHINGS

FURNITURE & ART, Gothersgade 5. Tel. 33/12-15-30.

Margit Smith has assembled two floors of streamlined Danish

contemporary design. Take a look even if it's too big for your suitcase.

ILLUMS BOLIGHUS, Amagertorv 10 (Strøget). Tel. 33/14-19-41.

The center of modern Danish design, it claims "only the best is good enough" and fills four floors with displays of the finest kitchenware, tableware, lamps, carpets, textiles, and furniture, including the creations of acclaimed Danish designers Hans Wegner, Borge Mogensen, Le Klint, and Arne Jacobsen. The store ships all over the world.

LYSBERG, HANSEN & THERP, Bredgade 3. Tel. 33/14-47-87.

Just off Kongens Nytorv, this shop features an extensive collection of beautifully designed Danish furniture, home accessories, and lighting.

NOTRE DAME, Nørregade 7. Tel. 33/15-17-03.

Practical rather than trendy, and always crowded, it features a large selection of items for the home, including eggcups, candles and candleholders, picture frames, dishclothes, cutlery, canisters, glasswear, ribbons, toys, bath items, and baskets.

KITCHENWARE

BODUM, Østergade 26 (Strøget). Tel. 33/91-77-44.

This is the place for tea kettles, cups, thermoses, ice buckets, salad bowls, and those famous "plunger pots" for coffee—all sleekly designed. Sale items—if you're so lucky—represent impressive savings.

SAXKJAERS, Købmagergade 53. Tel. 31/11-07-77.

Streamlined Danish tea and coffee pots, thermoses, cutlery, and ceramics fill this shop in the Latin Quarter, at the corner of Peder Hvitfeldts Stræde.

JEWELRY

THE AMBER SPECIALIST, Frederiksberggade 2 (Strøget). Tel. 33/11-88-03.

Amber, called "the gold of the north," is actually petrified resin from the coniferous forests that once covered Denmark. The trees are gone, but the amber still regularly washes ashore and is crafted into striking necklaces, rings, earrings—all available in this well-stocked store.

BRORSON DESIGN, Gråbrødre Torv 5.

Eye-catching costume jewelry is available here from $5 up.

GEORG JENSEN, Østergade 40. Tel. 31/11-40-80.

Known worldwide for its fine silver creations, Jensen's has everything from jewelry to watches to cutlery, not to mention a museum, at Bredgade 4 (tel. 33/12-45-55).

MUSEUMS KOPI SMYKKER, Gronnegade 6. Tel. 33/32-76-72.

If you like jewelry that doubles as a conversation piece, check out this array of museum reproductions of Scandinavian jewelry from the Bronze Age through the Crusades: pendants, brooches, arm rings, rings, bracelets, scarf buckles, earrings, necklaces, beads, coins, and amulets. They come in gold, silver, bronze, and gold-plated bronze. The shop has a branch at the Copenhagen Airport, beside the walkway to gates 27 to 41 (tel. 31/50-03-10).

MARKET

COPENHAGEN FLEA MARKET, Israels Plads.

This bustling open-air market, specializing in antiques and bric-a-brac, is open every Saturday from May to October between 8am and 2pm. Other days, you can buy fruits, vegetables, and flowers here. Take the S-tog to Nørreport and come early for the best bargains.

PEWTER

THE PEWTER CENTRE, 2 Ny Østergade. Tel. 33/14-82-00.

Just off Strøget behind Hotel d'Angleterre, there's as much pewter assembled under one roof as you're likely to see anywhere. In fact, it's the most extensive assortment in Scandinavia, collected from 16 different countries. Some of it has a shiny finish and looks remarkably like silver.

POSTCARDS

KØBENHAVN SOUVENIR, Frederiksberggade 28.

The selection of cards is good, so's the quality. Better still, they cost 1 Kr (.20¢) instead of the usual 5 Kr (.90¢). The place is open fairly late, until 8pm weeknights and 7pm on Saturday and Sunday.

POSTERS

POSTER LAND, Nygade 7 (Strøget).

It claims the largest assortment of posters and reproductions in northern Europe—good possibilities for souvenirs and gifts.

SHOPPING COMPLEX

SCALA, Axeltorv 2 and Vesterbrogade. Tel. 33/15-12-15.

The shops in this multilevel complex are on the ground floor, interspersed with fast-food eateries. On the other levels you'll find restaurants and a multiplex cinema. The frequent, free live music makes browsing here especially pleasant.

TOYS

Toys are sold at **Notre Dame** (see "Furniture and Home Furnishings," above). In addition, there's:

KREA, Vestergade 4–6. Tel. 33/32-98-58.

Don't forget the kids. This centrally located toy shop, a block north of Strøget not far from Town Hall, sells toys that are not only clever and colorful, they're educational, too. Besides Lego bricks, you'll find lots of typically Danish wooden toys.

CHAPTER 9

COPENHAGEN NIGHTS

When you see hundreds of lively revelers crowd Strøget until sunrise on a warm summer night, you realize how much the Danes love their nights—and all that goes on during them. But this is not to say that evening entertainment in Copenhagen is only for the young; jazz clubs, traditional beer houses, and wine cellars are routinely packed with people of all ages. The city has a serious cultural side, too, exemplified by the excellent theaters, operas, and ballets.

Half-price tickets for concerts and theater are available the same day of the performance from the ticket kiosk opposite the Nørreport rail station, at Nørre Voldgade and Fiolstræde. It's open Monday through Friday from noon to 7pm and Saturday from noon to 3pm.

On summer evenings there are outdoor concerts in Fælled Park near the entrance near Frederik V's Vej; inquire about dates and times at the tourist office.

1. THE PERFORMING ARTS

THEATER, OPERA & BALLET

THE ROYAL THEATER (Det Kongelige Teater), Kongens Nytorv. Tel. 33/14-10-02 after 1pm.

Copenhagen's cultural scene is dominated by a single theater, the

MAJOR CONCERT AND PERFORMANCE HALL BOX OFFICES

Mermaid Theater, Skt. Peders Stræde 27. Tel. 33/11-43-03.

The Royal Theater (Det Kongelige Teater), Kongens Nytorv. Tel. 33/14-10-02.

Tivoli Concert Hall, Vesterbrogade 3. Tel. 33/15-10-01.

Royal Theater, one of the few places in the world regularly staging theater, opera, and ballet under the same roof. Founded in 1748, the theater alternates productions between its two stages. Regular premieres and popular revivals keep the stage lit almost every night of the season.

Prices: 40–230 Kr ($7–$40.35); half price for those under 26 and over 67 years old.

Open: Box office, Sept–May Mon–Sat 1–8pm. **Closed:** June–Aug and Sun. **Directions:** At the south end of Kongens Nytorv.

MERMAID THEATER, Skt. Peders Stræde 27. Tel. 33/11-43-03 from noon to 4pm.

It is known for English-language stage plays. Performances usually star British or American actors.

Prices: 55–75 Kr ($9.65–$13.15) benches, 95–110 Kr ($16.65–$19.30) chairs.

Open: Usually Mon–Sat at 8pm; check the daily newspapers or ask the tourist board for current schedules and show times.

TIVOLI CONCERT HALL, Vesterbrogade 3. Tel. 33/15-10-01.

Tivoli's fifth concert hall, this one opened in 1956 and hosts soloists, conductors, orchestras, choirs, ballet, modern dance, and opera. The theater seats 2,000. The Tivoli Symphony often performs here during the four-month season. About half of the performances are free. Note that a ticket to a concert does not include admission to Tivoli but a ticket of admission to Tivoli does include a free concert, if one is scheduled for that night—a tremendous saving since admission to Tivoli is low to begin with. An added pleasure is that the entrance to the concert hall is through the lovely Tivoli gardens.

Prices: 150–250 Kr ($26.30–$43.85), but many events are free.

Open: Box office, Mon–Sat noon–6pm; also on Sun when events are scheduled. Performances generally at 7:30 or 9pm. **Closed:** Third week in Sept to third week in Apr.

2. THE CLUB & MUSIC SCENE

JAZZ, BLUES & ROCK

Copenhagen's love affair with jazz and blues is the most passionate in Europe. Danes have wholeheartedly embraced jazz as their own, and even though this capital's clubs are not as plentiful as those in New Orleans or Chicago, they challenge the American variety in both quality and enthusiasm.

MONTMARTRE, Nørregade 41. Tel. 33/13-69-66.

Montmartre is the self-proclaimed center of the Danish jazz scene, supporting live music nightly from 9:30pm to 1am. Miles Davis, Stan Getz, Dizzy Gillespie, and Oscar Peterson have all performed here, as have the best Danish jazzmen. After hours on weekend nights, dance discs spin until 5am.

Piano concerts are given in adjacent Café Monten on Tuesday, Wednesday, and Thursday afternoons.

Admission: Concerts 50–250 Kr ($8.80–$43.85) depending on the performer; disco 45 Kr ($6.90).

Open: Mon–Fri 11am–5am, Sat–Sun 8pm–5am.

BEN WEBSTER, Vestergade 7. Tel. 33/93-88-45.

Some of the best jazz in town is performed nightly at the far end of this intimate cellar restaurant, with white brick walls and glowing candles. On Monday, 20 musicians are in attendance. Come for drinks—figure 20 to 30 Kr ($3.50 to $5.25) per drink, dinner (out of budget range, though), or the disco, which takes over at 1am.

Admission: 30 Kr ($5.25) for jazz; 20 Kr ($3.50) for the disco.

Open: Daily 6pm–3am.

DE TRE MUSKETERER, Nicolaj Plads. Tel. 33/12-50-67.

This is another top jazz club featuring traditional styles. Bopping along for more than 20 years, the Three Musketeers attracts an upbeat, middle-aged crowd with its easy atmosphere and good dance floor.

Admission: 35–70 Kr ($6.15–$12.30).

Open: Tues–Thurs 8pm–1:30am, Fri–Sat 8pm–2:30am, Sun 3–6pm.

CA'FEEN FUNKE, Sankt Hans Torv. Tel. 31/35-17-41.

This small local favorite is rarely visited by tourists. Live bands usually perform on Monday, Wednesday (jazz), and Saturday (blues and funk). Best of all, there's never a cover charge. Arrive early if you want to sit.

Admission: Free.

Open: Daily 11am–2am; music usually starts at 8pm. **Bus:** No. 5, 14, or 16 from Nørreport to Blegdamsvej; look for the blue facade.

DIN'S, Lille Kannikestræde 3. Tel. 33/93-87-87.

Din's is a restaurant and bar with a very active stage. Although rock bands sometimes perform here, the intimate back room is best suited to the jazz and blues performances held weeknights except Tuesday, which is devoted to stand-up comedy. On weekends, rock-and-roll takes center stage. The music starts at 11:30pm.

Admission: 20 Kr ($3.50), which includes a beer.

Open: Mon–Thurs 4pm–1am, Fri 4pm–4am, Sat 2pm–4am.

HAND I HANKE, Griffenfeldsgade 20. Tel. 31/37-20-70.

Blues and rock are the main agenda at this local bar with board floors, wooden tables and benches, and plants in the windows. All ages feel at home here. The music takes place downstairs, hanging out and playing backgammon upstairs. There's a bar menu, and a backgammon tournament is held every Sunday for 15 Kr ($2.65).

Admission: 25–45 Kr ($4.40–$7.90), depending on the band; price includes a beer or glass of wine.

Open: Daily 2pm–2am. **Bus:** No. 5, 7, or 16 to Nørreport.

BOHEMIAN HANGOUTS

HUSET (The House), Rådhusstræde 13. Tel. 33/32-00-66.

A Copenhagen phenomenon, this active student information, entertainment, and cultural center attracts students and alternative folks of all ages to its clubs, restaurant, café, theater, cinema, and video gallery with 80 selections. **Musikcafeen** features top jazz and rock bands nightly; **Bar Bue** goes in for live punk, rap, and New Wave music during the week, disco on weekends; **Kafe Par Zalu** (a spoof on Port Salud), a lively weekend meeting spot for people in their early 20s, often has a live band (usually jazz) on Sunday afternoons. By contrast, **Cafe Rosa Luxemburg,** named after the German revolutionary and founder of the Spartacus League, is a small, quiet bar.

Admission: Free to 50 Kr ($8.80), depending on the band.

Open: Daily 10am–2am; call or drop by for specific hours of its individual entities.

FREE ENTERTAINMENT

SCALA, Axeltorv 2. Tel. 33/15-12-15.

Open since 1989, the modern, multilevel Scala center has become a magnet for shopping, dining, entertainment, and people-watching. Numerous balconies provide a spot to stand or sit and enjoy the wide range of talented musicians who perform everything from jazz to classical guitar to pop several times a day on the second-level balcony. Or hop in one of the glass-enclosed elevators and observe the colorful scene as you glide up and down the airy atrium. Performance schedules are posted at the ground level.

Admission: Free.

Open: 7am–1am. Entertainment is usually at lunchtime and interspersed throughout the afternoon and evening.

DISCO

As in other major cities, dance clubs come and go as fast as hiccups, and once gone, are just as quickly forgotten. If you're really into this scene, ask around and check the local glossy giveaways (available in most clubs and record stores). Below is a tried-and-true option.

U-MATIC, Vestergade 10. Tel. 33/32-88-00.

This good late-night dance club is owned by the adjacent Krasnapolsky (see below). A long bar runs along one wall, leaving just enough room for the tables and dance floor. Most important, the sound is good, and there are several video screens. It has a good DJ, attracts an arty crowd, and offers some gay evenings.

Admission: Thurs 25 Kr ($4.40), Fri–Sat 50 Kr ($8.80); other nights free or 30 or 40 Kr ($5.25 or $7), depending on scheduled events.

Open: Tues–Sat 11pm–4:30am.

GAY CLUBS

CAFE PAN AND DISCO, Knabrostræde 3. Tel. 33/32-49-08.

The café has a relaxed atmosphere and comfortable surroundings, and serves snacks and sandwiches all day, while in the disco there's dancing till the wee hours. Thursday nights are for women only. It's conveniently located half a block from Strøget.

Admission: Sun 10 Kr ($1.75), Mon–Tues free, Wed–Thurs 30 Kr ($5.25), Fri–Sat 55 Kr ($9.65).

Open: Café, Sun–Tues 1pm–3am, Wed–Thurs 1pm–2am, Fri–Sat 1pm–5am; disco Sun–Thurs 10pm–3am, Fri–Sat 10pm–5am.

PINK CLUB, Farvergade 10. Tel. 33/11-26-07.

This large, popular bar attracts primarily gay men.

Admission: Free.

Open: Daily 4pm–4am.

CAFE BABOOSHKA, Turensensgade 6. Tel. 33/15-05-36.

It's one of the few clubs in town primarily for lesbians.

Admission: Free.

Open: Daily 11am–midnight.

JEPPES KLUB 48, Allegade 25. Tel. 31/87-32-48.

Open for dancing one night a week, it draws a lesbian crowd. The women often end the evening at Café Intime next door (see below).

Admission: Free.

Open: Fri only, 9pm–3am.

CAFE INTIME, Allegade 25. Tel. 31/34-19-58.

True to its name, this intimate, inviting place with a piano draws everyone: gay men, lesbians, and heterosexuals.

Admission: Free.

Open: Daily 4pm–2am.

COSY BAR, Studiestræde 24. Tel. 33/12-74-27.

The last stop of the evening on the gay circuit because of the late hours it keeps, it attracts mainly gay male night owls.

Admission: Free.

Open: Sun–Thurs 11pm–6am, Fri–Sat 11pm–7am.

3. THE BAR SCENE

"IN" SPOTS

KRASNAPOLSKY, Vestergade 10. Tel. 33/32-88-00.

This popular restaurant and bar, with minimal decor and a pool table in back, can be laid-back and low-key or loud and boisterous. Drinks are served from a long well-stocked bar. For many, Krasnapolsky is just a way to warm up before visiting U-Matic disco, next door.

Prices: Mixed drinks 32–48 Kr ($5.60–$8.40).

Open: Mon–Sat 10am–2am, Sun 3pm–2am.

CAFE DAN TURRELL, St. Regnegade 3–5. Tel. 33/14-10-47.

Opened in 1977 and named after the contemporary Danish author of westerns and murder mysteries, it attracts art and architecture students and other young intellectuals, who converse intently over cheeseburgers, pastrami sandwiches, and chili. Turrell's dust jackets decorate the wall behind the bar and neon slashes the ceiling. It's easy to imagine James Dean propped at one end of the bar.

Prices: 34–44 Kr ($5.95–$7.70).

Open: Daily 11am–1:45am; kitchen closes at 10pm.

CAFE VICTOR, Ny Østergade 8. Tel. 33/13-36-12.

Cafe Victor serves crêpes, quiches, and omelets to laid-back, hardworking locals. Ceiling-to-floor windows look onto the street, and singles and sightseers often drink or enjoy a small meal at the 1950s-style bar.

Prices: Beer and wine 20 Kr ($3.50).

Open: Mon–Sat 9am–2am.

PEDER OXE VINKÆLDER, Gråbrødre Torv 11. Tel. 33/11-11-93.

Both unabashedly upbeat and terminally crowded, the Vinkælder's basement bar is one of the best in the city. The bulk of the crowd is too young to afford dinner at the popular and expensive restaurant above. Weekend nights require a strong voice to be heard over the music and the crowd.

Prices: Beer 20 Kr ($3.50); mixed drinks 39 Kr ($6.85).

Open: Daily noon–1am.

IMPRESSIONS

After all, the Danes are a people of some piety. They can forget food and women for a short period. . . .

—FROM AN ACCOUNT OF A DANISH VIKING VICTORY OVER NORWEGIAN VIKINGS IN IRELAND

OLD-TIME BEER HALL & BARS

VIN AND ØLGOD, Skindergade 45. Tel. 33/13-26-25.

Vin and Ølgod is to Copenhagen what the Hofbrauhaus is to Munich. Served by the half liter (about $6.50), beer is the drink of choice here, with emphasis on quantity. Oom-pah bands pump out all the drinking standards, from "Roll Out the Barrel" to "Wonderful, Wonderful Copenhagen," and revelers are encouraged to sing along (usually off-key) and dance (cheek-to-cheek or on the tables). Vin and Ølgod is spirited and just good fun. The hall is centrally located, between Strøget and Købmagergade.

Admission: 25 Kr ($4.40) Mon–Thurs, 50 Kr ($8.80) Fri–Sat.

Open: Mon–Sat 8pm–2am.

VINSTUEN 90'EREN, Gammel Kongevej 90. Tel. 31/31-84-90.

This place is for beer lovers. If you think you've tried them all, belly up to this bar and order Fadøl, a creamy, frothy beer that's like no other. A half liter of draft takes so long to pour (about 15 minutes) that patrons are advised to order a bottle of Carlsberg while waiting for the heavy foam to subside. The 76-year-old bar attracts everyone from dispirited drunkards to artists and actors (often one and the same).

Prices: Half liter of Fadøl 33 Kr ($5.80).

Open: Mon–Wed 10am–1:30am, Thurs–Sat 10am–2am, Sun and holidays noon–1:30am.

HVIIDS VINSTUE, Kongens Nytorv 19. Tel. 33/15-10-64.

This is Copenhagen's most historic wine cellar, faithfully serving citizens since 1723. It's no miracle that Hviids is still open as it's a great place to drink. The large crowd of locals and visitors always includes a good share of the audience from the Royal Theater across the street. One cozy seating area leads to another.

Prices: Beer and wine 19 Kr ($3.35).

Open: Daily 10am–1am. **Closed:** Sun May–Aug.

NYHAVN SAILORS' BAR

The sailors are now far outnumbered by landlubbers, but this bar still captures the spirit of the area's peppery port past.

NYHAVN!, Nyhavn 17. Tel. 33/12-54-19.

Boisterous sing-alongs are led by a lively organist and singer tipping the scales at 300 pounds (135 kg). Paintings of sailors and women overlook the dance floor, which gets crowded on Friday and Saturday nights.

Prices: Beer 20 Kr ($3.50), whisky 22 Kr ($3.85).

Open: Tues–Sun, music from 8pm.

4. MORE ENTERTAINMENT

TIVOLI, Vesterbrogade 3. Tel. 33/15-10-01.

Besides its outstanding concerts (see "The Performing Arts," above), Tivoli is thrilling for the fireworks displays on Wednesday, Friday, and Saturday nights. And there's no better way to wile away an evening than strolling through its magnificent grounds, ablaze with 110,000 lights.

Prices: 28 Kr ($4.90) for adults, 14 Kr ($2.45) for children if you arrive before 1pm; half price for children under 12. Rides cost 10–15 Kr ($1.75–$2.65).

Open: Third week in Apr to third week in Sept, daily 10am–midnight. Fireworks flare at 11:30pm.

MOVIES

Copenhagen is a movie city, and most films are in English with Danish subtitles. The going price of a ticket is about 55 Kr ($9.65), but in some places, such as **Palads** (the building near the Scala Center that looks like a psychedelic wedding cake and features 19 small cinemas), you pay only 30 or 40 Kr ($5.25 or $7) for features that begin before 6pm and on Monday nights. Independent cinemas include **Delta Bio,** Kompagnistræde 19 (tel. 33/11-76-03), and **Klaptræet,** Kultorvet 11 (tel. 33/13-00-09).

GAMBLING

CASINO COPENHAGEN, SAS Scandinavia Hotel, Amager Boulevard 70. Tel. 33/11-23-24.

Denmark's first fully licensed casino opened December 31, 1990, with blackjack, roulette, and baccarat. The casino is run by Casinos Austria International, the world's largest casino operator.

Admission: 40 Kr ($7).

Open: Daily 4pm–4am or until the last gambler heads home.

CHAPTER 10

EASY EXCURSIONS FROM COPENHAGEN

The outings in this chapter are not only convenient, they're quick—even the one to Sweden. You can leave Copenhagen in the morning, do some adventuring, and be back in the city by late afternoon or early evening.

The essential, not-to-be-missed excursion from Copenhagen leads to the **Louisiana Museum of Modern Art,** in Humlebæk. It's Denmark's most-visited museum, set in a sculpture garden along the Danish coast. The train ride takes half an hour; come back by bus along the scenic coast road (for more information, see "The Top Attractions" in Chapter 6).

For more extended travels outside Copenhagen, consider the **Danish State Railway (DSB) "Special Excursion" ticket,** which includes Louisiana but also farther-flung tourist draws such as Legoland, every child's dream-come-true, as well as Odense, the birthplace of Hans Christian Andersen (see "Cool for Kids" in Chapter 6).

HELSINGØR (ELSINORE)

"Four-hundred years of legal piracy," from the 15th through the 19th century, made Helsingør rich from tolls assessed on passing ships. Today, a walk around this carefully restored old town is proof enough that this was at one time Denmark's most important parcel. A wonderful architectural legacy and other indelible marks have been made on this seaside village by traders from around the world. But Helsingør is most famous for its 16th-century **Kronborg Castle** (tel. 49/21-30-78), a regal structure that some claim William Shakespeare had in mind while penning *Hamlet.* Whether or not this is true, it is inarguable that the castle is nothing less than majestic.

IMPRESSIONS

Something is rotten in the State of Denmarke.
—SHAKESPEARE, *HAMLET*

The interior is notably empty of furnishings, many of them having been consumed in a large blaze in December 1859, when King Frederik VII had the castle fires banked a bit too high.

The castle tour features the royal apartments, the ballroom, the chapel, and other ancient areas. Located on the Danish coast, 28 miles north of Copenhagen, Helsingør may be reached by train from Central Station in about an hour.

The castle is open May through September, daily from 10:30am to 5pm; in April and October, daily from 11am to 4pm; and the rest of the year, daily from 11am to 3pm. Admission is 16 Kr ($2.80) for adults, 8 Kr ($1.40) for children. Joint admission to the castle and Maritime Museum is 26 Kr ($4.55) for adults, half price for children. A visit in August might even coincide with a production of *Hamlet.*

Other places of interest in Helsingør include **Saint Mariæ convent,** founded in 1430, and **Marienlyst Palace,** which once was home to Dowager Queen Juliane Marie in the 18th century and now houses the town's museum. Also of note is an 18th-century **mansion** with 11 bay windows at Strandgade 95. It, like many houses in Helsingør, has sash windows, a bow to English architecture rarely found in Denmark. One of the town's oldest houses, **The Anchor,** at Strandgade 27, was built in 1577.

Færgestræde (Ferry Street) is a narrow, picturesque street stretching from the harbor square to Stengade (Stone Street) and lined with 17th-century houses.

Swedes often cross the Øresund (Sound) to Helsingør to take advantage of the lower prices here. This is one of the rare places in Denmark that accepts Swedish crowns.

RUNGSTEDLUND

A visit to Rungstedlund, 25km (15 miles) north of Copenhagen and the home of writer and baroness **Karen Blixen** (alias Isak Dinesen, 1885–1962), may easily be combined with a trip to Kronborg Castle or the Louisiana Museum of Modern Art (above). Dinesen was the author of *Seven Gothic Tales, Winter Tales,* and the autobiographical *Out of Africa,* among other works, and twice a nominee for the Nobel Prize for Literature.

The house and belongings were opened to the public in May 1991. Blixen's parents purchased the property, the 18th-century Rungsted Inn, in 1875, and the author was born here 10 years later. After living and managing a coffee plantation in Africa from 1914 to 1931, she returned to Rungsted and the family home, where she lived until her death in 1962. Her grave is on the grounds beneath a marker that says simply "Karen Blixen."

Visitors enter the museum through the old barn, which now

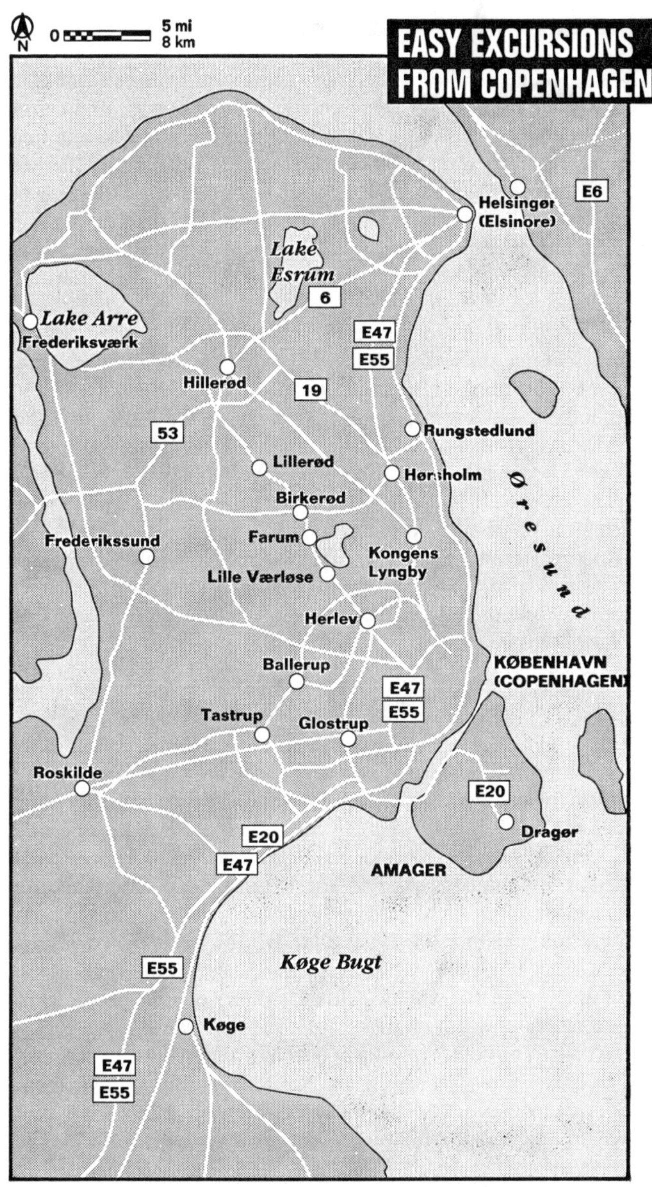

IMPRESSIONS

I cannot help but think how much better I have been understood and accepted in America than in Denmark.

—Isak Dinesen, after the publication of her first book, *Seven Gothic Tales*

houses a gallery, a library filled with editions of Dinesen's books, a theater showing audiovisual presentations about her life and career (headphones for English or Danish), a bookshop, and a café and adjoining garden. In the main house, it appears as if Dinesen has just stepped away for a moment. The Green Room is filled with many of the belongings she brought back from Africa, including the favorite wicker chair of her lover, Denys Finch Hatton, who died tragically in a plane crash, and the old phonograph he gave her (featured prominently in the film *Out of Africa).*

In Ewald's Room, named after Johannes Ewald, author of the Danish national anthem, who stayed in the house when it was an inn, Dinesen wrote many of her stories on the modest Corona typewriter. The house's drawing room was the scene in the 1950s of radio broadcasts of the famous storyteller recounting her tales. (By the way, Dinesen's home in Kenya is also open to the public, but is hauntingly empty compared to its Danish counterpart; the Dinesen family chose to keep the possessions in one place.)

Another claim to fame for Rungsted: Norwegian composer Edvard Grieg visited the village in 1865 and composed his piano sonata in E minor and violin sonata in F major here.

Take the train from Copenhagen to Rungsted Kyst.

ROSKILDE

For centuries, Danish kings and queens have been laid to rest at the redbrick, twin-spired **cathedral** in Roskilde, most recently King Frederik IX in 1985. Today people visit the town, which lies due west of Copenhagen and a half-hour train ride away, primarily to see the cathedral and royal tombs and the **Viking Ship Museum,** on Strandengen. Open daily, the museum houses five ships raised from the Roskilde Harbor in 1962. Purposefully sunk as barricades around A.D. 1000, they include two warships, two merchant ships, and a small vessel that was used either as a ferry or fishing boat. Films in English about the excavation of the ships are shown.

The **main square** of Roskilde becomes a fruit, flower, vegetable, and flea market on Wednesday and Saturday mornings. Its **palace,** which now houses a collection of paintings and furniture from local merchant families, was built in 1733; the **town hall,** in 1884. The **tourist office** (tel. 42/35-27-00) is located near the cathedral.

In summer, excursion boats ply the **Roskilde Fjord,** and concerts are held throughout the venerable town, as well as in **Roskilde Park** on Tuesday nights. At the end of June, Roskilde hosts a popular, annual three-day **beat, rock, and jazz festival** that is the largest in northern Europe and attracts top performers.

If you come for the festival, try to book lodging ahead. The town has hotels, motels, inns, bed-and-breakfast accommodations, a youth hostel (open mid-May to the end of August), and camping, as well as car and bicycle rentals. For more information, inquire at the tourist office (tel. 42/35-27-00).

Trains (and buses no. 123 and 210) run frequently between Copenhagen and Roskilde; if you choose to explore the area further, take the bus from Roskilde 6 miles (10km) west to **Lejre** and the **Historical Archeological Research Center.** Every summer the 42-acre (17-ha) reconstructed village here comes alive as it was 2000 years ago, when Vikings inhabited the region. Children can talk with the "inhabitants," try out some of the Iron Age tools and utensils, and sail in a dugout canoe.

MALMÖ, SWEDEN

Sweden's third largest city—undeniably modern but with a 13th-century core—lies directly across the channel from Copenhagen. It's possible to zip over to Malmö from Copenhagen in 45 minutes by hydrofoil; by ferry, it's 90 minutes. Both services depart from Havnegade, at the corner of Nyhavn, in Copenhagen; be sure to pack your passport.

The ferry costs 55 Kr ($9.65) one way. The hydrofoil, or *flyvebadene* (tel. 33/12-80-88), costs 89 Kr ($14.75) each way (half price for children under 16). Senior citizens are entitled to a special one-day round-trip fare of 42 Kr ($7.35), but they are relegated to travel between 6am and 3pm.

Visitors to Malmö particularly enjoy the architecture in the old part of the town, as well as the **Malmö Museum** in Malmöhus, a 15th-century castle. The city has several parks (one is surrounded by water, another is the largest in Sweden), an inviting 4.2-mile (7km) stretch of sandy beach, and a youth hostel. The **Tourist Office** is at Hamngatan 1 (tel. 040/34-12-70; room-booking service, tel. 040/34-12-68); ask about the value-packed Malmö Card, good for one or more days.

If you'd like to stay longer, consider the DSB's two-day **Around the Sound,** excursion ticket to Sweden and back via boat and train. It's double the fun.

APPENDIX

A. BASIC PHRASES & VOCABULARY

Hello	**Goddag**	go *da*
How are you?	**Hvordan har De det?**	vohr-*dahn* haar dee day
Very well	**Godt**	tak gaht
Thank you	**Tak**	tak
Goodbye	**Farvel**	fahr-*vel*
Please	**Vær så venlig**	vayr saw *ven*lee
Yes	**Ja**	ya
No	**Nej**	nai
Excuse me	**Undskyld**	*own*-skeel
I don't understand	**Jeg forestår ikke**	vai fawr-*star* ik-uh
Give me . . .	**Giv mig . . .**	Gee-mai
Where is . . . ?	**Hvor er der . . . ?**	vohr ayr der
the train station	**banegården**	bæ*ner*-*gawr*en
a hotel	**et hotel**	it ho-tel
a restaurant	**en restaurant**	in rest-oh-*rahng*
the toilet	**toilettet**	twah-*let*-tud
To the right	**Til hojre**	till hoi-ruh
To the left	**Til venstre**	till ven-struh
I would like . . .	**Jeg vil gerne have . . .**	yai-vil-luh *gayr*-nuh-ha
to eat	**noget at spise**	noh-ud ah spee-suh
a room	**et værelse**	it *vay*-rul-suh
How much is it?	**Hvor meget?**	vohr *ma*-yud
When?	**Hvornaar?**	vohr-*nawr*
Yesterday	**i går**	ee gawr
Today	**i dag**	ee da
Tomorrow	**i morgen**	ee *maw*rn
Write it out	**Skriv det**	*skreev* day

1 **en** (ayn)
2 **to** (toh)
3 **tre** (tray)
4 **fire** (*feer*-ah)
5 **fem** (fem)
6 **seks** (sex)
7 **syv** (syee)
8 **otte** (*oh*-tuh)
9 **ni** (nee)
10 **ti** (tee)
11 **elleve** (*el*-vuh)
12 **tolv** (tahll)
13 **tretten** (*tret*-un)

14 **fjorten** (*fyawr*-tun)
15 **femten** (*fem*-tun)
16 **seksten** (*saiss*-tun)
17 **sytten** (*ser*-tun)
18 **atten** (*a*-tun)
19 **nitten** (*ni*tun)
20 **tyve** (*tee*-vuh)
30 **tredive** (*tred*-vuh)
40 **fyrre** (*fer*-raw)
50 **halvtreds** (*hal*-tress)
60 **tres** (tress)
70 **halvfjerds** (half-*yayrss*)
80 **firs** (feerss)
90 **halvfems** (hal*femss*)
100 **hundrede** (*hoon*-rud-uh)

B. MENU SAVVY

SOUPS

Aspargesuppe Asparagus soup
Blomkaalsuppe Cauliflower soup
Gule aerter Pea soup

EGGS

Aeggekage Omelet
Blødkogt aeg Soft-boiled egg
Hardkogt aeg Hard-boiled egg
Roraeg Scrambled eggs
Spejlaeg Fried egg

FISH

Al Eel
Fiske frikadeller Fish cakes
Hellefynder Halibut
Hummer Lobster
Krabber Crab
Krebs Crayfish
Laks Salmon
Makrel Mackerel
Muslinger Mussels
Orred Trout
Pighvar Turbot
Rejer Shrimp
Rodspaette Plaice
Sild Herring
Torsk Cod

MEATS

Agerhons Partridge
And Duck
Andesteg Roast duck
Bof Steak
Boller Meatballs
Due Pigeon
Dyr Venison
Fasan Pheasant
Flaeskesteg Roast pork
Gaas Goose
Hakkebof Hamburger
Kalkun Turkey
Kalve Veal
Kalvesteg Roast veal
Kylling Chicken
Lam Lamb

Lammesteg Roast lamb
Lever Liver
Leverpostej Liver pâté
Okse Beef
Oksesteg Roast beef
Polser Sausages
Skinke Ham
Spegepolse Salami
Svin Pork
Tunge Tongue
Vildand Wild duck

VEGETABLES

Aerter Peas
Agurk Cucumber
Asparges Asparagus
Blomkaal Cauliflower
Bonner String beans
Gulerodder Carrots
Hvidkal Cabbage
Kartofler Potatoes
Log Onions
Ris Rice
Rodkaal Red cabbage
Rosenkaal Brussels sprouts
Tomater Tomatoes

FRUITS

Aebler Apples
Ananas Pineapple
Appelsiner Oranges
Blommer Plums
Ferskner Peaches
Hindbaer Raspberries
Jordbaer Strawberries
Paerer Pears

DESSERTS

Budding Pudding
Hindbaer med flode Raspberries with cream
Is Ice cream
Kompot Stewed fruit
Kager Pastry

BEVERAGES

Aeblemost Apple juice
Flode Cream
Kaffe Coffee
Maelk Milk
Ol Beer
Te Tea
Vand Water
Vin Wine

BASICS

Brod Bread
Ost Cheese
Salt Salt
Smor Butter

COOKING TERMS

Farseret Stuffed
Grilleret Grilled
Kogt Boiled
Ristet Fried
Stegt Roast

C. METRIC MEASURES

LENGTH

1 millimeter	=	0.04 inches (or less than ⅙ in)
1 centimeter	=	0.39 inches (or just under ½ in)
1 meter	=	1.09 inches (or about 39 inches)
1 kilometer	=	0.62 miles (or about ⅔ of a mile)

To convert kilometers to miles, take the number of kilometers and multiply by .62 (for example, 25km × .62 = 15.5 mi).

To convert miles to kilometers, take the number of miles and multiply by 1.61 (for example, 50 mi × 1.61 = 80.5 km).

CAPACITY

1 liter = 33.92 fluid ouncés or 1.06 quarts or 0.26 gallons

To convert liters to gallons, take the number of liters and multiply by .26 (for example, 50 liters × .26 = 13 gallons).

To convert gallons to liters, take the number of gallons and multiply by 3.79 (for example, 10 gal × 3.79 = 37.9 liters).

WEIGHT

1 gram	=	0.04 ounces (or about a paperclip's weight)
1 kilogram	=	2.2 pounds

To convert kilograms to pounds, take the number of kilos and multiply by 2.2 (for example, 75kg × 2.2 = 165 pounds).

To convert pounds to kilograms, take the number of pounds and multiply by .45 (for example, 90 lb × .45 = 40.5kg).

TEMPERATURE

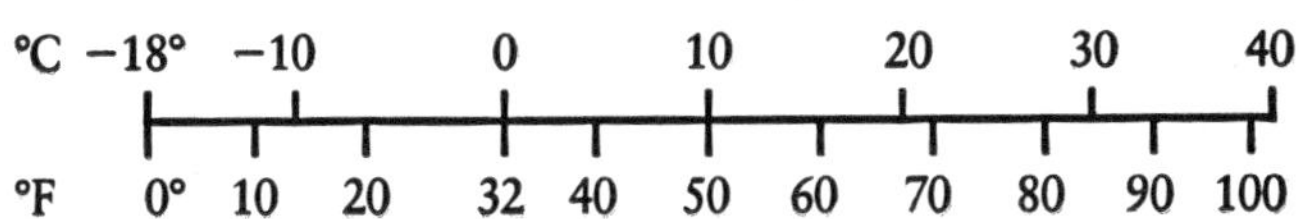

To convert degrees C to degrees F, multiply degreees C by 9, divide by 5, then add 32 (for example 9/5 × 20°C + 32 = 68° F).

To convert degrees F to degrees C, subtract 32 from degrees F, then multiply by 5, and divide by 9 (for example, 85°F − 32 × 5/9 = 29°C).

D. SIZE CONVERSIONS

The following charts should help you to choose the correct clothing sizes in Denmark. However, sizes can vary, so the best guide is simply to try things on.

WOMEN'S DRESSES, COATS & SKIRTS

American	3	5	7	9	11	12	13	14	15	16	18
Continental	36	38	38	40	40	42	42	44	44	46	48

WOMEN'S BLOUSES & SWEATERS

American	10	12	14	16	18	20
Continental	38	40	42	44	46	48

WOMEN'S STOCKINGS

American	8	8½	9	9½	10	10½
Continental	1	2	3	4	5	6

WOMEN'S SHOES

American	5	6	7	8	9	10
Continental	36	37	38	39	40	41

MEN'S SUITS

American	34	36	38	40	42	44	46	48
Continental	44	46	48	50	52	54	56	58

MEN'S SHIRTS

American	14½	15	15½	16	16½	17	17½	18
Continental	37	38	39	41	42	43	44	45

MEN'S SHOES

American	7	8	9	10	11	12	13
Continental	39½	41	42	43	44½	46	47

MEN'S HATS

American	6⅞	7⅛	7¼	7⅜	7½	7⅝
Continental	55	56	58	59	60	61

CHILDREN'S CLOTHING

American	3	4	5	6	6X
Continental	98	104	110	116	122

CHILDREN'S SHOES

American	8	9	10	11	12	13	1	2	3
Continental	24	25	27	28	29	30	32	33	34

INDEX

GENERAL INFORMATION

SIGHTS & ATTRACTIONS

NOTE: An asterisk (*) after an attraction name indicates that the attraction is an Author's Favorite.

ACCOMMODATIONS

KEY TO ABBREVIATIONS: *CG* = Campground; *D* = Dormitory; *PH* = room in Private Home; *W* = Worth the Extra Bucks; *YH* = Youth Hostel; *$* = Super Budget Choice; (*) = an Author's Favorite

RESTAURANTS

BY CUISINE

KEY TO ABBREVIATIONS: *W* = Worth the Extra Bucks; *$* = Super Budget Choice; (*) = an Author's Favorite

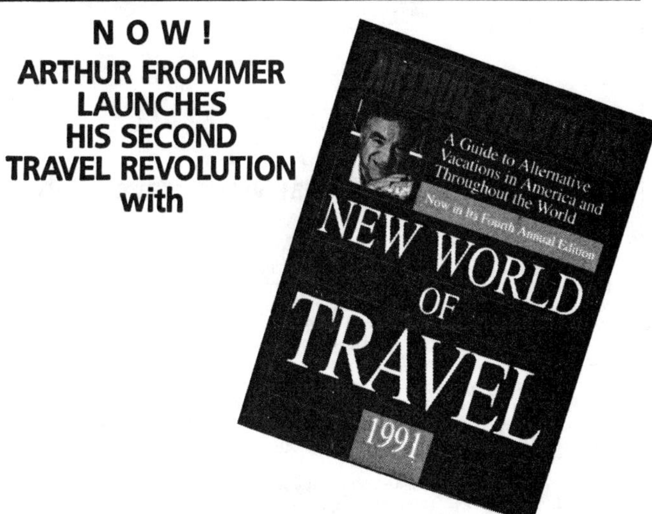

The New World of Travel

The hottest news and latest trends in travel today—heretofore the closely guarded secrets of the travel trade—are revealed in this new sourcebook by the dean of American travel. Here, collected in one book that is updated and expanded every year, are the most exciting, challenging, and money-saving ideas in travel today.

You'll find out about hundreds of alternative new modes of travel—and the many organizations that sponsor them—that will lead you to vacations that cater to your mind, your spirit, and your sense of thrift.

Learn how to fly for free as an air courier; travel for free as a tour escort; live for free on a hospitality exchange; add earnings as a part-time travel agent; pay less for air tickets, cruises, and hotels; enhance your life through cooperative camping, political tours, and adventure trips; change your life at utopian communities, low-cost spas, and yoga retreats; pursue low-cost studies and language training; travel comfortably while single or over 60; sail on passenger freighters; and vacation in the cheapest places on earth.

And in every yearly edition, Arthur Frommer spotlights the 10 GREATEST TRAVEL VALUES for the coming year. 448 pages, large-format with many, many illustrations. All for $16.95!

ORDER NOW

TURN TO THE LAST PAGE OF THIS BOOK FOR ORDER FORM.

NOW, SAVE MONEY ON ALL YOUR TRAVELS!

Join Frommer's™ Dollarwise® Travel Club

Saving money while traveling is never a simple matter, which is why the **Dollarwise Travel Club** was formed 31 years ago. Developed in response to requests from Frommer's Travel Guide readers, the Club provides cost-cutting travel strategies, up-to-date travel information, and a sense of community for value-conscious travelers from all over the world.

In keeping with the money-saving concept, the annual membership fee is low—$20 for U.S. residents or $25 for residents of Canada, Mexico, and other countries—and is immediately exceeded by the value of your benefits, which include:

1. Any TWO books listed on the following pages.
2. Plus any ONE Frommer's City Guide.
3. A subscription to our quarterly newspaper, *The Dollarwise Traveler.*
4. A membership card that entitles you to purchase through the Club all Frommer's publications for 33% to 40% off their retail price.

The eight-page ***Dollarwise Traveler*** tells you about the latest developments in good-value travel worldwide and includes the following columns: **Hospitality Exchange** (for those offering and seeking hospitality in cities all over the world); **Share-a-Trip** (for those looking for travel companions to share costs); and **Readers Ask . . . Readers Reply** (for those with travel questions that other members can answer).

Aside from the Frommer's Guides and the Gault Millau Guides, you can also choose from our Special Editions. These include such titles as ***California with Kids*** (a compendium of the best of California's accommodations, restaurants, and sightseeing attractions appropriate for those traveling with toddlers through teens); ***Candy Apple: New York with Kids*** (a spirited guide to the Big Apple by a savvy New York grandmother that's perfect for both visitors and residents); ***Caribbean Hideaways*** (the 100 most romantic places to stay in the Islands, all rated on ambience, food, sports opportunities, and price); ***Honeymoon Destinations*** (a guide to planning and choosing just the right destination from hundreds of possibilities in the U.S., Mexico, and the Caribbean); ***Marilyn Wood's Wonderful Weekends*** (a selection of the best mini-vacations within a 200-mile radius of New York City, including descriptions of country inns and other accommodations, restaurants, picnic spots, sights, and activities); and ***Paris Rendez-Vous*** (a delightful guide to the best places to meet in Paris whether for power breakfasts or dancing till dawn).

To join this Club, simply send the appropriate membership fee with your name and address to: Frommer's Dollarwise Travel Club, 15 Columbus Circle, New York, NY 10023. Remember to specify which single city guide and which two other guides you wish to receive in your initial package of member's benefits. Or tear out the next page, check off your choices, and send the page to us with your membership fee.

FROMMER BOOKS
PRENTICE HALL PRESS
15 COLUMBUS CIRCLE
NEW YORK, NY 10023
212/373-8125

Date____________________

Friends:

Please send me the books checked below.

FROMMER'S™ GUIDES

(Guides to sightseeing and tourist accommodations and facilities from budget to deluxe, with emphasis on the medium-priced.)

- ☐ Alaska. $14.95
- ☐ Australia $14.95
- ☐ Austria & Hungary $14.95
- ☐ Belgium, Holland & Luxembourg $14.95
- ☐ Bermuda & The Bahamas $14.95
- ☐ Brazil $14.95
- ☐ Canada $14.95
- ☐ Caribbean $14.95
- ☐ Cruises (incl. Alaska, Carib, Mex, Hawaii, Panama, Canada & US). . $14.95
- ☐ California & Las Vegas. $14.95
- ☐ Egypt $14.95
- ☐ England & Scotland. $14.95
- ☐ Florida $14.95
- ☐ France. $14.95
- ☐ Germany $14.95
- ☐ Italy $14.95
- ☐ Japan & Hong Kong. $14.95
- ☐ Mid-Atlantic States $14.95
- ☐ New England $14.95
- ☐ New Mexico. $13.95
- ☐ New York State. $14.95
- ☐ Northwest. $16.95
- ☐ Portugal, Madeira & the Azores. $14.95
- ☐ Scandinavia $18.95
- ☐ South Pacific $14.95
- ☐ Southeast Asia $14.95
- ☐ Southern Atlantic States $14.95
- ☐ Southwest. $14.95
- ☐ Switzerland & Liechtenstein. $14.95
- ☐ USA $16.95

FROMMER'S $-A-DAY® GUIDES

(In-depth guides to sightseeing and low-cost tourist accommodations and facilities.)

- ☐ Europe on $40 a Day. $15.95
- ☐ Australia on $40 a Day $13.95
- ☐ Costa Rica; Guatemala & Belize on $35 a Day $15.95
- ☐ Eastern Europe on $25 a Day . $16.95
- ☐ England on $50 a Day $13.95
- ☐ Greece on $35 a Day. $14.95
- ☐ Hawaii on $60 a Day $14.95
- ☐ India on $25 a Day $12.95
- ☐ Ireland on $35 a Day $13.95
- ☐ Israel on $40 a Day $13.95
- ☐ Mexico on $35 a Day. $14.95
- ☐ New York on $60 a Day $13.95
- ☐ New Zealand on $45 a Day. $14.95
- ☐ Scotland & Wales on $40 a Day. $13.95
- ☐ South America on $40 a Day. $15.95
- ☐ Spain on $50 a Day $15.95
- ☐ Turkey on $30 a Day $13.95
- ☐ Washington, D.C. & Historic Va. on $40 a Day $13.95

FROMMER'S TOURING GUIDES

(Color illustrated guides that include walking tours, cultural and historic sites, and other vital travel information.)

- ☐ Amsterdam $10.95
- ☐ Australia $10.95
- ☐ Brazil $10.95
- ☐ Egypt $8.95
- ☐ Florence $8.95
- ☐ Hong Kong $10.95
- ☐ London. $10.95
- ☐ New York. $10.95
- ☐ Paris $8.95
- ☐ Rome $10.95
- ☐ Scotland $9.95
- ☐ Thailand $10.95
- ☐ Turkey. $10.95
- ☐ Venice. $8.95

(TURN PAGE FOR ADDITONAL BOOKS AND ORDER FORM)

0391